SYMBOLIC ANALYSIS FOR PARALLELIZING COMPILERS

SYMBOLIC ANALYSIS FOR PARALLELIZING COMPILERS

Mohammad R. HAGHIGHAT
Center for Supercomputing Research and Development
University of Illinois at Urbana-Champaign
Urbana, Illinois, USA

KLUWER ACADEMIC PUBLISHERS
Boston/London/Dordrecht

Distributors for North America:
Kluwer Academic Publishers
101 Philip Drive
Assinippi Park
Norwell, Massachusetts 02061 USA

Distributors for all other countries:
Kluwer Academic Publishers Group
Distribution Centre
Post Office Box 322
3300 AH Dordrecht, THE NETHERLANDS

Library of Congress Cataloging-in-Publication Data

A C.I.P. Catalogue record for this book is available
from the Library of Congress.

Copyright © 1995 by Kluwer Academic Publishers

All rights reserved. No part of this publication may be reproduced, stored in a retrieval system or transmitted in any form or by any means, mechanical, photocopying, recording, or otherwise, without the prior written permission of the publisher, Kluwer Academic Publishers, 101 Philip Drive, Assinippi Park, Norwell, Massachusetts 02061

Printed on acid-free paper.

Printed in the United States of America

To Shahin, Leila, and Roxanna

CONTENTS

FOREWORD		xvii
PREFACE		xxi
ACKNOWLEDGMENTS		xxiii
1	**INTRODUCTION**	1
	1.1 Contributions	2
	1.2 Book Outline	3
2	**RELATED WORK**	5
3	**SYMBOLIC ANALYSIS**	9
	3.1 Abstract Symbolic Domain	13
	3.2 Abstraction of the Assignment Operation	14
	3.3 Abstraction of Integer Division	15
	3.4 Tests of Integer Divisibility	16
	3.5 Interpretation of Flow Graph Nodes	21
	3.6 Interpretation of Program Loops	23
4	**INDUCTION VARIABLES**	35
	4.1 Generalized Induction Variables	37

4.2	Generalized Induction Expressions	40
4.3	Symbolic Interpolation	46
4.4	Induction Expressions with Conditional Statements	50
4.5	Wraparound Expressions	51
4.6	Loop Normalization	54
4.7	Recognition of Loop-Invariant Computations	55
4.8	Architecture of A Symbolic Analysis System	56

5 INTERPROCEDURAL SYMBOLIC ANALYSIS 59
- 5.1 Dead-Code Elimination 61
- 5.2 Symbolic Dependence Analysis 63
- 5.3 Program Optimization 68

6 TIMING ANALYSIS AND SCHEDULING 71
- 6.1 Loop Scheduling 72
- 6.2 Derivation of Symbolic Cost Estimates 78
- 6.3 Computing Probabilities of Structural Conditions 82
- 6.4 Algebra of Conditional Values 84

7 IMPLEMENTATION AND EXPERIMENTS 93

8 CONCLUSIONS 95
- 8.1 Future Research 95

A INTERVAL ANALYSIS 97
- A.1 Introduction 97
- A.2 The Origin of Interval Analysis 98
- A.3 Interval Arithmetic 99
- A.4 Extended Interval Arithmetic 101

A.5 Interval Functions 103
A.6 Intervals in Aid of Program Analysis 110

REFERENCES 115

INDEX 135

LIST OF FIGURES

Chapter 3

3.1	Algebraic properties of integer arithmetic.	11
3.2	Algebraic properties of symbolic arithmetic.	12
3.3	Algebraic properties of integer division.	15
3.4	Proof of integer divisibility of $n^2 + n$ by 2 by induction.	17
3.5	Finding the abstract function of a flow graph node.	22
3.6	Transformation of a code segment by Parafrase-2.	22
3.7	Finding the abstract function of a loop.	24
3.8	Non-nested, non-disjoint loops are merged together.	26
3.9	Normalization of nested loops that share header.	27
3.10	Loop analysis in a case with cyclic dependences.	28
3.11	A loop with cyclic recurrence relations.	30
3.12	Unsolvability of the loop termination problem.	30
3.13	Example of analysis of loop termination by Parafrase-2.	31
3.14	Analysis of a loop with multiple exits.	32
3.15	Loop bounds may be modified within the loop.	33

Chapter 4

4.1	Example of linear induction variable substitution.	35
4.2	Linear induction variables in trapezoidal loops.	36
4.3	Parafrase-2 recognizes generalized induction variables.	38
4.4	A code segment extracted from program TRFD.	39
4.5	Induction analysis of the code segment of Figure 4.4.	39

4.6	An induction expression recognized by Parafrase-2.	41
4.7	Undecidability of the induction expression problem.	41
4.8	Induction analysis of a code segment of MDG.	43
4.9	Parallelization of a code segment of SPEC77.	45
4.10	Example of a nonlinear induction variable.	48
4.11	Symbolic Computation Tree of an expression.	49
4.12	Parafrase-2 recognizes conditional induction variables.	50
4.13	Wraparound variables recognized by Parafrase-2.	52
4.14	Wraparound variables in program TRFD.	53
4.15	Selective normalization of loop bounds.	55
4.16	Loop-invariant expressions recognized by Parafrase-2.	56
4.17	Symbolic analysis system of Parafrase-2.	57

Chapter 5

5.1	Interprocedural symbolic analysis of Parafrase-2.	60
5.2	Dead-code elimination performed by Parafrase-2.	62
5.3	Generalized strength reduction of Figure 4.5.	69

Chapter 6

6.1	Adjoint-convolution program and its parallel work.	73
6.2	Gauss-Jordan program and its parallel work.	74
6.3	A loop partition to chunks of equal workload.	75
6.4	A transformation that balances workload.	76
6.5	Dynamic load balancing of a parallel loop.	77
6.6	Performance of various scheduling schemes.	78
6.7	Timing analysis of a Cholesky decomposition.	79
6.8	A code segment and its associated convex polytopes.	81
6.9	A nested loop and its iteration space.	83
6.10	The *truth* and *unit step* functions.	85
6.11	A loop nest with conditional statements.	89

List of Figures xiii

    6.12 A code fragment with conditional values.   91

Appendix A

    A.1 Interval arithmetic.   99
    A.2 Algebraic properties of interval arithmetic.   102
    A.3 Integer powers of intervals.   105
    A.4 The lattice $\mathbb{R}$.   111

LIST OF TABLES

Chapter 5

5.1 Symbolic terms in Perfect Benchmarks®.   65

Chapter 7

7.1 Symbolic analysis capabilities of compilers.   94

FOREWORD

With this book, Mohammad Haghighat provides the first complete account of symbolic analysis techniques and their impact on parallelizing compiler technology.

Professor David Kuck and his colleagues at the University of Illinois pioneered research on automatic program vectorization and parallelization in the early 70s by laying out the foundation of what was to become the most important component of parallel processing. For almost the next two decades, Kuck's group, along with Professor Ken Kennedy's group at Rice University and Fran Allen's group at IBM, dominated the field.

Research activities on parallelizing compilers grew exponentially during the last 6-7 years, drawing a tremendous number of researchers into the field. This growth coincided with the wide-spread proliferation of parallel computers and applications and promised a panacea for the complexities of parallel programming, and for ever increasing performance. Although enormous progress has been made, to this date parallelizing compilers remain complex and limited in what they can do and, as a result, expectations have become more realistic. It is fair to say that many of the leap steps forward happened during the early research activities on parallelizing compilers; it is indicative that dependence analysis techniques which were developed by Dr. Utpal Banerjee in the late 70s are at the core of the latest experimental and commercial parallelizing compilers.

Through his research work, which started in 1988, Mohammad Haghighat pioneered a new approach for dependence analysis and program optimization. Based on earlier concepts of symbolic analysis and abstract interpretation, he designed, developed, and prototyped a novel unifying framework for dependence analysis and optimization. His approach solved problems that were long-considered fundamental bottlenecks in the Fortran world (such as complex induction variable substitution). It is worth noting that when Dr. Haghighat started his research work on symbolic analysis and optimization, virtually no other activity in the parallelizing compilers community was similar to it; the closest cousins were ad hoc pattern matching techniques for recognizing specific forms for induction variables, or restricted cases of dependences. The fact that symbolic analysis has now become an integral part of all major compiler research efforts is a testament to the impact his work has had on our community during the last 4-5 years. Despite the growth of research activities and the importance of symbolic analysis on parallelizing compilers, Dr. Haghighat's approach remains the most powerful and complete tool available to date.

This book gives a refined and detailed version of this important work by an author who is most qualified to write about the state-of-the-art on symbolic analysis. It is also the first such monograph on symbolic analysis and parallelization. The author does an excellent job demonstrating the effectiveness of symbolic analysis in tackling important optimization problems, some of which are also inhibitors to loop parallelization. In particular, the framework presented in this book has proven extremely successful on induction and wrap-around variable analysis, strength reduction, dead code elimination, and symbolic constant propagation. The symbolic analysis approach presented in this book can be applied to any program transformation or optimization problem that makes use of properties and value ranges of program names.

The author has implemented the techniques discussed in this book on Parafrase-2, a widely used experimental compiler developed at the University of Illinois. The results of his implementation and experiments not only demonstrate the importance of symbolic analysis in optimization and parallelization, but they also disprove skeptics' main concern, namely the efficiency and complexity of the approach. Symbolic

Foreword xix

analysis can be useful to any transformational system or optimization problem that relies on compile-time information about program variables; this covers virtually the majority, if not all, optimization and parallelization techniques.

This book makes a compelling case for the potential of symbolic analysis by applying it for the first time, and with remarkable results, to a number of classical optimization problems: loop scheduling, static timing or size analysis, and dependence analysis. The book demonstrates how symbolic analysis can solve these problems faster and more accurately than existing hybrid techniques.

With encouraging evidence and growing hope that symbolic analysis might indeed be the panacea we all anticipate, I expect that this book will become a very important resource and guide to researchers, students, and compiler writers in industry and academia.

Constantine D. Polychronopoulos

PREFACE

The notion of dependence captures the most important properties of a program for efficient execution on high-performance computers. The dependence structure of a program defines the necessary constraints of the order of execution of the program components, and provides sufficient information for the exploitation of the available parallelism and locality. Static discovery and management of the dependence structure of programs save a tremendous amount of execution time, and dynamic utilization of dependence information results in a significant performance gain on parallel computers.

However, experiments with parallel computers indicate that existing multiprocessing environments are unable to deliver the desired performance over a wide range of real applications, mainly because of lack of precision of their dependence information. This calls for an effective compilation scheme capable of understanding the dependence structure of complicated application programs.

This book describes a methodology for capturing and analyzing program properties that are essential in the effective detection and efficient exploitation of parallelism on parallel computers. Based on this methodology, a symbolic analysis framework is developed for the Parafrase-2 parallelizing compiler. This framework extends the scope of a variety of important program analysis problems and solves them in a unified way. The attained solution space of these problems is much larger than that handled by the existing compiler technology. Such a powerful approach is required for the effective compilation of a large class of application programs.

ACKNOWLEDGMENTS

This book is based on my Ph.D. dissertation submitted to the Department of Computer Science at the University of Illinois at Urbana-Champaign. I owe an enduring debt of gratitude and appreciation to my thesis advisor, Constantine Polychronopoulos, for his guidance, support, encouragement and friendship. Constantine has been both a source of inspiration and a model of mentorship, and I can only hope that this work approaches the high standard of excellence of his own works. I am also thankful to my dissertation committee members, Samuel Kamin, David Kuck, Dennis Mickunas, and David Padua, for their invaluable time and insightful comments.

Outside of my thesis committee, I thank the following people without whom the process of completing this work would not have been as pleasurable as it has been: Utpal Banerjee and Mehdi Harandi for their guidance and support; Milind Girkar, Chia Ling Lee, Bruce Leung, and Dale Schouten, my fellow graduate students in the Parafrase-2 project, for their intellectual cooperative efforts; Jay Hoeflinger and Greg Jaxon for their expertise with supercomputer benchmarks; Merle Levy and Gail Pieper for proofreading an early draft of this book; José Moreira for the use of his simulator; and John Andrews, Carl Beckmann, Georgios Dimitriou, José Moreira, and Hideki Saito for invigorating group discussions.

I am indebted to my professors at Shiraz University, Majid Azarakhsh, Hassan Eghbali, Mohammad Hassan Kadivar, Seradjeddin Katebi, Mohammad Ali Mobarhan, Mohammad Moradi, and Ahmad Towhidi, for their early intellectual support and encouragement.

My heartfelt thanks are reserved for my first dear teachers, my parents.

1
INTRODUCTION

High performance on parallel computers can be achieved only when they are programmed effectively. The complexity of this task and portability issues make automatic support of parallel program development highly desirable [AK87, FERN84, KKLW80, PW86, Pol88]. Despite all the effort spent on the automatic parallelization of programs, existing parallelizing compilers are not able to deliver the desired performance over a wide range of real applications [BE92]. The challenging problem confronting designers of parallelizing compilers is the difficulty of collecting sufficient information in an efficient way to utilize the underlying architecture.

This book describes a methodology for the discovery of certain program properties that are essential in the effective detection and efficient exploitation of parallelism. Based on this methodology, we have built a compiler analysis framework for Parafrase-2 [PGH$^+$89], a source-to-source multilingual parallelizer developed at the University of Illinois. Within this framework, symbolic analysis is used as an abstract interpretation technique to solve a variety of interprocedural flow analysis problems in a unified way.

We studied the effectiveness of our techniques on the Perfect Benchmarks® [Bea89], a suite of Fortran programs representative of real engineering and scientific codes. Problematic cases, identified by other studies on automatic parallelization [EHJ+91, EHLP91, SH92], were the focus of our experimentation. We also studied performance of three of the state-of-the-art parallelizing compilers: Cedar Fortran compiler, based on a 1991 version of KAP, from Kuck and Associates [Kuc88]; the Titan 1500/3000 compilation system from Kubota Pacific Computer Inc.; and the Alliant FX/Fortran compiler, based on VAST-2 preprocessor, found in [CDL88]to be one of the best commercial vectorizers. In this book we do not attempt a comparative study of these compilers, but instead, we focus on cases from real applications where the techniques employed by these compilers were ineffective. The attained solution space of these problems in our framework was much larger than that handled by the existing compiler technology. In particular, our symbolic analyzer was able to automatically solve the most complicated cases of induction analysis identified in [EHJ+91, EHLP91, SH92].

Problems that are solved interprocedurally in our symbolic analysis framework include symbolic constant propagation, generalized induction variable substitution, global forward substitution, and detection of loop invariant computations. These problems have a vital role in dependence analysis [All83, Ban88, Wol89], the fundamental component of parallelizing compilers. Some of the analytical tools used effectively in our compilation scheme are mathematical methods such as computer algebra, calculus of finite differences, and theorem proving techniques based on number theory. Such a powerful combined approach is required for the effective compilation of a large class of application programs, as demonstrated by our implementation and experimental results.

1.1 CONTRIBUTIONS

The main contribution of this work is a methodology for capturing and analyzing program properties that are essential in the effective detection and efficient exploitation of the available parallelism. These properties are about factors that have a critical role in the structure of computations performed by programs. These include the relationships between problem size, loop bound expressions, array subscript expressions, and their effects on a program's execution time. Based on this methodology, a compiler analysis framework has been built for Parafrase-2 [PGH+89]. This framework extends the scope of a variety of important program analysis problems, and solves them in a unified way. The attained solution space of these problems is well out of reach of the existing compiler technology. It is also shown that such a powerful combined approach is required for the effective compilation of a large class of application programs. Some of the solved problems are:

- Accurate computation and efficient propagation of symbolic expressions.
- Recognition of generalized induction expressions.
- Detection of loop-invariant computations.
- Aggressive dead-code elimination as a result of interprocedural analysis.
- Dependence analysis in presence of unknown variables.
- Cost analysis of programs.
- Scheduling schemes guided by symbolic timing analysis.
- Generalized strength reduction over nest of parallel and sequential loops.

1.2 BOOK OUTLINE

This book is organized as follows. Chapter 2 briefly discusses the related work. The methodology of symbolic analysis is described in Chapter 3. Chapter 4 focuses on induction variables and their importance for parallelizing compilers. Various issues in interprocedural analysis and optimization are studied in Chapter 5. Application of symbolic analysis in computing program cost estimates and using the derived cost estimates to guide the scheduling of parallel loops are described in Chapter 6. Implementation of this work in the frame of Parafrase-2, and comparison of capabilities of Parafrase-2 with some of the state-of-the-art parallelizing compilers are summarized in Chapter 7. Concluding remarks and directions for future research are presented in Chapter 8. Appendix A gives a brief review of the theory of interval analysis and its application in the abstract analysis of computer programs.

2

RELATED WORK

Early work on data flow analysis was done by Allen, Cocke, and Schwartz among others [CS70]. Kennedy [Ken81]gives a survey of data flow analysis techniques. In his pioneering work on semantics of programming languages, Scott [Sco72]outlined a general theory of finite approximation with the aid of lattice theory. The theory provides a strong foundation for construction of a variety of data-type spaces which can be used for semantic interpretation of programming languages. Sintzoff [Sin72]showed that a property of a program may be verified by computing the program in a model corresponding to that property in which values are abstract objects and functions are mappings on these objects. The Cousots were the first to propose an abstract interpretation framework for systematic flow analysis [CC76, CC77, CC79, Cou81]. In a recent paper [CC92], they survey various abstract interpretation frameworks.

Constant propagation has been extensively studied in the literature in the context of global flow analysis, and is used in all optimizing and parallelizing compilers. While the constant propagation problem is undecidable in general [RL86], there are conservative algorithms that find subsets of constants in programs. Kildall in his lattice-theoretic approach to data flow analysis [Kil73]presented a general iterative algorithm for distributive frameworks that converges to the *maximum fixed point solution*of the problems.

Reif and Lewis [RL77] used a sparse data structure, called *Global Value Graph*, to find the same information that can be found by Kildall's algorithm, but in a more efficient way. Reif and Tarjan [RT81] employed Global Value Graph to obtain *covers*; mappings from text expressions to symbolic expressions that are useful in program optimization techniques. Cytron *et al.* [CCF91, CFR$^+$89, CFR$^+$91] have presented techniques for efficient computation of *static single assignment*(SSA) intermediate form. Alpern, Wegman, and Zadeck [AWZ88] presented an algorithm for detecting many of the statically detectable classes of equalities by translating the programs into SSA intermediate form. The SSA form of a program facilitates the recognition of equivalences among program expressions that are not lexically identical[RWZ88].

Wegbreit [Weg75b] showed how *symbolic interpretation* can be used to determine properties from a *well-founded property set*. Wegman and Zadeck [WZ84, WZ85, WZ91] presented an efficient method for constant propagation when conditional branches are taken into consideration. Their algorithm does a form of constant propagation in combination with dead code elimination to find the same class of constants that can be found by Wegbreit's method. Grove and Torczon [GT93] have studied various implementations of jump functions for solving the interprocedural constant propagation problem.

Cheatham et al. [CHT79] and Clarke and Richardson [CJ81a, CJ81b, CR85] have studied symbolic evaluation techniques with an emphasis on their applications in program verification and testing.

Induction variable detection, as a basis for *strength reduction*, has been extensively studied in the literature [ASU86, ACK81, CK77a, CS70, FU76, Pai81, PS77]. *Induction variables substitution*, the inverse of strength reduction, is used to eliminate the parallelism-inhibiting dependences that are the result of the way induction variables are defined and used [AK87, Wol78, ZC91]. In a study on compiling C programs for parallel execution, Allen and Johnson [AJ88] discussed induction variable substitution and presented a heuristic solution for

RELATED WORK

forward substitution that is implemented in the Titan compiler. The notion of *generalized induction variables* was introduced by Eigenman *et al.* [EHJ+91, EHLP91] in their study on parallelization of Perfect Benchmarks®. Automatic recognition of generalized induction variables has been independently studied by Wolfe [Wol92] and by us [HP92].

Recently, there has been an increasing number of research focused on semantics-based static analysis of programs. Jouvelot and Dehbonei [JD89] presented a unified approach for the parallelization of generalized reductions. They have also studied partial symbolic evaluation as a formalism for semantical interprocedural analysis of imperative programs [DJ92]. Ammarguellat and Harrison [AHI90] used abstract interpretation to automatically recognize induction variables and recurrence relations by matching them with patterns from a table of recurrence templates. Field [Fie92] has presented a formal rewriting system for reasoning about imperative programs. Havlak [Hav93, Hav94] has studied techniques for efficient representation and analysis of symbolic values.

3
SYMBOLIC ANALYSIS

We are interested in the set V of program variables and constants with integer type. The ring $\mathbb{Z}$ of integers is an *integral domain*; that is, a commutative ring with multiplication identity that satisfies the cancellation law. Hence, if the value of a syntactic expression e at a state s of a program is represented by $\mathcal{E}[\![e]\!]s$, then the properties shown in Figure 3.1 hold.

The values of program variables are not available at compile time, yet a technique is required to statically discover properties of programs to be exploited by optimizing and parallelizing compilers. This can be achieved by specifying the relationship between actual values and their descriptions, and by establishing a connection between the operations on the actual values and those on the corresponding abstract values. This theory of semantics approximation is called *abstract interpretation* [CC77, CC79, CC92]. The term approximate does not imply any possibilities of incorrectness, but rather the lack of full information is meant. Roughly speaking, in the method of abstract interpretation the compiler employs an interpreter to execute programs in an abstract domain, in order to discover their properties.

There is a clear tradeoff between the level of abstraction and the precision of the analysis. In the design of the mappings between concrete and abstract values, a guiding principle is the efficiency of abstract operations; in particular, the abstract *equality* operation has a key role. Since many compiler optimization problems require the capability of verification or discovery of equality relationship between expressions of programs, it is desirable to make the abstract equality operation as efficient as possible. An efficient way to decide whether two objects are equal is to decide whether their representing data structures are *identical*. However, axioms of the integral domain $\mathbb{Z}$, described above, indicate the existence of equal but not identical arithmetic expressions such as $(i+j)*(i-j)$ and i^2-j^2. This suggests a *canonical* system in which equivalent objects have unique representations. In fact, there are two main reasons for having a canonical representation system. First, efficient procedures can be built for carrying out operations on the objects when they are in a canonical form. Second, the *zero equivalence* problem, that is, the problem of deciding equivalence between two objects, is immediately solved when equivalent objects have identical representations.

Richardson [Ric68] has shown that the zero equivalence problem is recursively unsolvable for a sufficiently rich class of transcendental expressions. Theoretical limitations and other unsolvability results concerning transcendental terms in computer algebra may be found in [BL82, Cav70, Mos71]. The zero equivalence problem, however, can be solved in many cases of practical interest. In particular, the case of polynomials does not pose any difficulties.

There is a variety of choices for canonical representation of polynomials [DST93, GCL92]. We represent multivariate polynomials in a *sparse distributive* canonical form using the *lexicographical ordering* of program variables. In this form, only non zero elements are represented, with the exception of *zero* polynomial. For example, $j*(3k+2i)$ will be represented as $2ij + 3jk$. Later, we shall discuss the necessary modifications of this form to handle symbolic division operation and also to take care of side effects of operations that cannot be precisely abstracted. In the distributive representation all variables forming a polynomial are given the same importance, unlike the *recursive* rep-

Commutativity:	$\forall i, j \in V$, $\mathcal{E}[\![i+j]\!]s = \mathcal{E}[\![j+i]\!]s = \mathcal{E}[\![i]\!]s + \mathcal{E}[\![j]\!]s$, $\mathcal{E}[\![i*j]\!]s = \mathcal{E}[\![j*i]\!]s = \mathcal{E}[\![i]\!]s * \mathcal{E}[\![j]\!]s$.
Associativity:	$\forall i, j, k \in V$, $\mathcal{E}[\![i+(j+k)]\!]s = \mathcal{E}[\![(i+j)+k]\!]s$, $\mathcal{E}[\![i*(j*k)]\!]s = \mathcal{E}[\![(i*j)*k]\!]s$.
Distributivity:	$\forall i, j, k \in V$, $\mathcal{E}[\![i*(j+k)]\!]s = \mathcal{E}[\![(i*j)+(i*k)]\!]s$.
Identities:	$\forall i \in V$, $\mathcal{E}[\![i+0]\!]s = \mathcal{E}[\![i]\!]s$, $\mathcal{E}[\![i*1]\!]s = \mathcal{E}[\![i]\!]s$.
Inverse:	$\forall i \in V$, $\mathcal{E}[\![i-i]\!]s = \mathcal{E}[\![0]\!]s$.
Cancellation:	$\forall i, j, k \in V$, $\mathcal{E}[\![i]\!]s \neq \mathcal{E}[\![0]\!]s$, $\mathcal{E}[\![i*j]\!]s = \mathcal{E}[\![i*k]\!]s \Rightarrow \mathcal{E}[\![j]\!]s = \mathcal{E}[\![k]\!]s$.

Figure 3.1 Algebraic properties of integer arithmetic.

Commutativity:	$\forall a, b \in E,$ $\mathcal{S}[\![a+b]\!]e \doteq \mathcal{S}[\![b+a]\!]e \doteq \mathcal{S}[\![a]\!]e \oplus \mathcal{S}[\![b]\!]e,$ $\mathcal{S}[\![a*b]\!]e \doteq \mathcal{S}[\![b*a]\!]e \doteq \mathcal{S}[\![a]\!]e \circledast \mathcal{S}[\![b]\!]e.$
Associativity:	$\forall a, b, c \in E,$ $\mathcal{S}[\![a+(b+c)]\!]e \doteq \mathcal{S}[\![(a+b)+c]\!]e,$ $\mathcal{S}[\![a*(b*c)]\!]e \doteq \mathcal{S}[\![(a*b)*c]\!]e.$
Distributivity:	$\forall a, b, c \in E,$ $\mathcal{S}[\![a*(b+c)]\!]e \doteq \mathcal{S}[\![(a*b)+(a*c)]\!]e.$
Identities:	$\forall a \in E,$ $\mathcal{S}[\![a+0]\!]e \doteq \mathcal{S}[\![a]\!]e,$ $\mathcal{S}[\![a*1]\!]e \doteq \mathcal{S}[\![a]\!]e.$
Inverse:	$\forall a \in E,$ $\mathcal{S}[\![a-a]\!]e \doteq \mathcal{S}[\![0]\!]e.$
Cancellation:	$\forall a, b, c \in E,\ \mathcal{S}[\![a]\!]e \neq \mathcal{S}[\![0]\!]e,$ $\mathcal{S}[\![a*b]\!]e \doteq \mathcal{S}[\![a*c]\!]e \Rightarrow \mathcal{S}[\![b]\!]e \doteq \mathcal{S}[\![c]\!]e.$

Figure 3.2 Algebraic properties of symbolic arithmetic.

resentation where a multivariate polynomial is treated as a univariate polynomial in a dominant variable whose coefficients are polynomials in other variables. Certain operations such as division can be performed more efficiently when polynomials are represented recursively. For such cases this transformation will be performed automatically in the process of abstract interpretation of those operations.

3.1 ABSTRACT SYMBOLIC DOMAIN

The objects in our abstract symbolic domain are canonical symbolic expressions. A canonical symbolic expression is a lexicographically ordered sequence of symbolic terms. Each symbolic term is in turn a pair of an integer coefficient and a sequence of pairs of pointers to program variables in the program symbol table and their exponents. The latter sequence is also lexicographically ordered. For example, the abstract value of the symbolic expression $2ij + 3jk$ is $((2, ((\uparrow^i, 1), (\uparrow^j, 1))), (3, ((\uparrow^j, 1), (\uparrow^k, 1))))$ in an environment that i is bound to $(1, ((\uparrow^i, 1)))$, j is bound to $(1, ((\uparrow^j, 1)))$, and k is bound to $(1, ((\uparrow^k, 1)))$. In our framework, *environment* is the abstract analogous of the *state* concept; an environment is a function from program variables to abstract symbolic values. Each environment e associates a canonical symbolic value e x for each variable $x \in V$; it is said that x is *bound* to e x. An environment could be represented by a list $\{x_1 \mapsto s_1, x_2 \mapsto s_2, \cdots, x_n \mapsto s_n\}$ in which exactly one symbolic value is associated with each variable. For the sake of clarity, in the following sections symbolic values are studied in their canonical form rather than the data structure level.

Given a syntactic arithmetic expression a and an environment e, the value of the expression in the environment can be determined. Thus, the meaning of syntactic arithmetic expressions can be defined as a total function S that takes two arguments: a syntactic construct and an environment. The canonical symbolic value of the arithmetic expression a in the environment e is denoted by $S [\![a]\!] e$. If E is the set of the syntactic arithmetic expressions of a program, and $\ominus$, $\oplus$, $\ominus$, and $\circledast$ are the abstract symbolic operations analogous to the concrete operations $=, +, -,$ and $*$, then the properties shown in Figure 3.2 hold. The important point evident from these relations is that no precision is lost in the process of symbolic interpretation, as far as integer arithmetic properties are concerned.

3.2 ABSTRACTION OF THE ASSIGNMENT OPERATION

An assignment operation has the form x = E, where x is a variable and E an expression. The assignment x = E in an environment e is abstracted by evaluating the symbolic value of the expression E in e, and then assigning that value to the variable x. All the variables take their most recently assigned values from the environment e, and the assignment creates a new environment. We shall assume that all the operations in the expression E are defined for their arguments. The order of evaluation is specified by the semantics of the programming language and is particularly important when operations might have side effects. Expressions involving procedure calls with side effects are examples of such cases.

The effect of a sequence of assignment operations is the functional composition of the effects of the individual assignments. Thus, a node of a control flow graph [ASU86] can be interpreted as an abstract operator which maps an input environment to an output environment. The abstract interpreter can determine the meaning of this operator from the assignments inside the node. Suppose that the sequence of assignment operations y = a * x; z = x * y − y; y = z/k; x = (2 * a * y)/z is to be executed in the environment $e_0 \stackrel{\text{def}}{=} \{a \mapsto a, k \mapsto 2, x \mapsto x, y \mapsto y, z \mapsto z\}$. The abstract interpreter can compute the resulting environment as follows:

$\mathcal{S}[\![$y = a * x; z = x * y − y; y = z/k; x = (2 * a * y)/z$]\!]e_0 =$
$(\mathcal{S}[\![$x = (2 * a * y)/z$]\!] \circ \mathcal{S}[\![$y = z/k$]\!] \circ \mathcal{S}[\![$z = x * y − y$]\!] \circ \mathcal{S}[\![$y = a * x$]\!])e_0 =$
$\mathcal{S}[\![$x = (2 * a * y)/z$]\!](\mathcal{S}[\![$y = z/k$]\!](\mathcal{S}[\![$z = x * y − y$]\!](\mathcal{S}[\![$y = a * x$]\!]e_0)))$

A new environment is created by each assignment operation.

$\mathcal{S}[\![$y = a * x$]\!]e_0 = \{a \mapsto a, k \mapsto 2, x \mapsto x, y \mapsto ax, z \mapsto z\} \stackrel{\text{def}}{=} e_1,$
$\mathcal{S}[\![$z = x * y − y$]\!]e_1 = \{a \mapsto a, k \mapsto 2, x \mapsto x, y \mapsto ax, z \mapsto ax^2 - ax\} \stackrel{\text{def}}{=} e_2,$
$\mathcal{S}[\![$y = z/k$]\!]e_2 = \{a \mapsto a, k \mapsto 2, x \mapsto x, y \mapsto (ax^2 - ax)/2, z \mapsto ax^2 - ax\} \stackrel{\text{def}}{=} e_3,$
$\mathcal{S}[\![$x = (2*a*y)/z$]\!]e_3 = \{a \mapsto a, k \mapsto 2, x \mapsto a, y \mapsto (ax^2 - ax)/2, z \mapsto ax^2 - ax\}.$

SYMBOLIC ANALYSIS

For all $k, m, n, p, q \in \mathbb{Z}$, $k \neq 0$, $n \neq 0$, $q \neq 0$:

(1) If $n|m$, then $kn|km$ and $\frac{km}{kn} = \frac{m}{n}$.

(2) If $n|m$ and $q|p$, then $nq|(mq+np)$ and $\frac{m}{n} + \frac{p}{q} = \frac{mq+np}{nq}$.

(3) If $n|m$ and $q|p$, then $nq|mp$ and $\frac{m}{n} \cdot \frac{p}{q} = \frac{mp}{nq}$.

Figure 3.3 Algebraic properties of integer division.

An important feature that an abstract interpreter must have in order to be able to carry on the above computations is the capability of symbolic division. Precise analysis of codes in which symmetric multidimensional arrays are stord in a compressed form depends on this capability.

3.3 ABSTRACTION OF INTEGER DIVISION

Let $m, n \in \mathbb{Z}$, $n \neq 0$. If there exists an integer k such that $m = nk$, then n *divides* m, and we write $n|m$. If n does not divide m, i.e. if there exists no integer k such that $m = nk$, we write $n \nmid m$. Let $r \in \mathbb{R}$ be the real division of m by n, i.e., $r = m/n$. The integer division of m by n, denoted by $\frac{m}{n}$, is defined to be $\lfloor r \rfloor$ if $r \geq 0$ and $\lceil r \rceil$ if $r < 0$. Note that $\frac{m}{n}$ is *not* the same as the *quotient* of m by n as defined in the field of rational numbers. In particular, observe that $n \cdot \frac{m}{n}$ is not necessarily equal to m, e.g., $2 \cdot \frac{1}{2} = 2 \cdot 0 = 0 \neq 1$. It is however equal to m if n divides m.

Given an integer division operation $\frac{p}{q}$, where p and q are two multivariate polynomials, if the interpreter can prove that q divides p for all the possible non zero values of q, then the abstract symbolic value of $\frac{p}{q}$ can be represented in a canonical form. Following are some equivalent integer division operations assuming that the denominators are not zero:

$$\frac{n^2-n}{2} = \frac{n-n^2}{-2} = \frac{2n^2-2n}{4} = \frac{n^3-n}{2n+2} = \frac{\frac{m^3n^2-m^3n-mn^2+mn}{12}}{\frac{m^3-m}{6}}.$$

The interpreter can use the algebraic properties of the integer division shown in Figure 3.3 to associate a unique abstract value to all the equivalent integer divisions. This canonical form is a pair of a numerator and a denominator. The numerator is a lexicographically ordered multivariate polynomial with integer coefficients and the denominator is a positive integer. Furthermore, no positive integer other than 1 may divide both the denominator and the coefficients of the numerator. Thus, the data structure for abstract symbolic values requires an extra field for representing an integer common denominator. In the following section, some techniques will be presented for deciding the divisibility of a polynomial by another one.

3.4 TESTS OF INTEGER DIVISIBILITY

Given two multivariate polynomials $\frac{p}{d_p}$ and $\frac{q}{d_q}$, where d_p and d_q are common denominators of the two polynomials, and p and q have integer coefficients, we need to determine whether the first polynomial is divisible by the second one. Using the first property of Figure 3.3, it can be shown that $\frac{p}{d_p}$ is divisible by $\frac{q}{d_q}$ if and only if $d_q p$ is divisible by $d_p q$. First, we try to find a polynomial p' with integer coefficients such that $p = p'q$. If such a polynomial does not exist, we conclude that $d_q p$ is not divisible by $d_p q$ and hence $\frac{p}{d_p}$ is not divisible by $\frac{q}{d_q}$. In the case that such a polynomial exists, the problem reduces to decision of divisibility of $d_q p'$ by an integer number d_q. Note that if such a polynomial p' exists, it will be unique and will be equal to the quotient of division of polynomial p by q.

If a multivariate polynomial is not divisible by another one, then the quotient and remainder of the division depends on which is considered

SYMBOLIC ANALYSIS

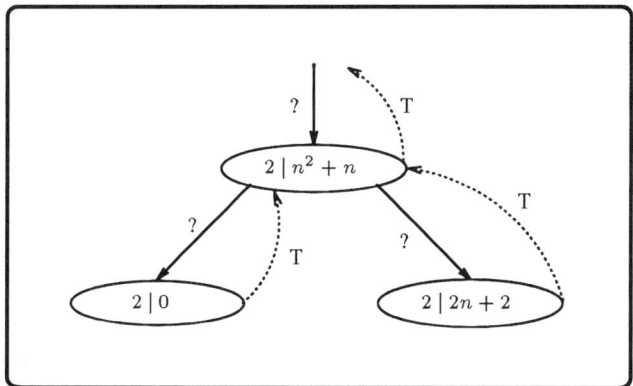

Figure 3.4 Proof of integer divisibility of $n^2 + n$ by 2 by induction.

as the main variable. For example, in the division of $ax + by$ by $x + y$, if x is the main variable, then the quotient is a and the remainder is $-ay + by$. But if y is the main variable, then the quotient is b and the remainder is $ax - bx$. However, if the denominator divides the numerator, then the remainder is zero and the quotient is unique, independent of the choice of the dominant variable. For example, the quotient of dividing $ax + ay$ by $x + y$ is a, regardless of whether x or y is considered as the main variable.

3.4.1 Integer Divisibility Test by Mathematical Induction

An effective test for the divisibility of a polynomial p by a non-zero integer n can be built using the principle of mathematical induction. First, the polynomial p and the integer n are simplified with respect to the greatest common divisor of the coefficients of p and n. If either n is equal to 1 or -1, or p is equal to 0, then the answer to the divisibility question is true. If p is a constant polynomial, then the divisibility of two integers is straightforward. Otherwise, the divisibility is tested by mathematical induction on value of v, one of the variables in the polynomial p.

In the induction basis, the divisibility by n is tested for p, simplified by substituting an arbitrary value for v, one of the variables in p. Zero is probably the most appropriate value, as it results in further simplification and efficient computation. For the induction step, the divisibility of p by n when $\text{v} \mapsto v + 1$ should be deduced from the hypothesis that p is divisible by n when $\text{v} \mapsto v$. We shall do so, by testing the divisibility of $\Delta p = [\![p]\!]\{\text{v} \mapsto v+1\} - [\![p]\!]\{\text{v} \mapsto v\}$ by n. In general, the degree of Δp is one less than that of p. If Δp is divisible by n, then by a bidirectional induction we have shown that p is divisible by n for all integers. Figure 3.4 shows the trace of proving the divisibility of $n^2 + n$ by 2 using mathematical induction. This method is capable of handling complicated multivariate polynomials.

3.4.2 Integer Divisibility Test by Limited Inspection

When the integer divisibility test is required, often the integer against which the divisibility is tested is a small number such as $2, 4$, or 6, that appears in the denominator of closed formulas of summations. In this section, we present a test for integer divisibility which is particularly efficient in these cases. This test is based on the following lemma.

LEMMA **3.4.1** *A polynomial $p(x)$ over $\mathbb{Z}$ is divisible by $k!$, $k \in \mathbb{N}$, if and only if $p(x)$ is divisible by $k!$ when x assumes a sequence of k consecutive integers.*

PROOF. Let n be the degree of p, and suppose that $k! | p(x), \forall x \in \{x_0, x_0+1, \cdots, x_0+k-1\}$. Consider the Newton's expansion [GKP89, Jor65] of p around x_0:

$$\begin{aligned} p(x) &= p(x_0) + \Delta p(x_0) \frac{(x-x_0)}{1!} + \cdots \\ &+ \Delta^n p(x_0) \frac{(x-x_0)(x-x_0-1)\cdots(x-x_0-n+1)}{n!}. \end{aligned}$$

$\Delta p(x)$ denotes the forward difference of p at x, and is equal to $p(x+1) - p(x)$. If n, the degree of p, is smaller than k, then values of p at the $n+1$ consecutive integers $\{x_0, x_0+1, \cdots, x_0+n\}$ uniquely determine the coefficients of p, and, by assumption, are all divisible by $k!$. In such a case, $\Delta p(x_0), \Delta^2 p(x_0), \cdots, \Delta^n p(x_0)$, that are successive differences of values of p at $\{x_0, x_0+1, \cdots, x_0+n\}$ will also be divisible by $k!$. In addition, in the mth term of the expansion, $\frac{(x-x_0)(x-x_0-1)\cdots(x-x_0-m+2)}{(m-1)!}$ is an integer, as the numerator is the product of $m-1$ consecutive integers, and hence, from an elementary theorem in number theory [NZM91], divisible by $(m-1)!$. Thus, $p(x)$ is divisible by $k!$ for all $x \in \mathbb{Z}$.

Now, assume that n, the degree of p, is greater than or equal to k. By a reasoning similar to that of the previous paragraph, it is concluded that $\Delta p(x_0), \Delta^2 p(x_0), \cdots, \Delta^{k-1} p(x_0)$ are divisible by $k!$. It remains to show that $k!$ also divides the other terms of the expansion, i.e. $\Delta^j p(x_0) \frac{(x-x_0)(x-x_0-1)\cdots(x-x_0-j+1)}{j!}, \forall j: k \leq j \leq n$.

Note that in the Newton's expansion of p around x_0, the term $\frac{\Delta^m p(x_0)}{m!}$ is an integer for all $m > 0$. The proof, which is based on the fact that p has integer coefficients, is as follows. The coefficient of x^n in p is $\frac{\Delta^n p(x_0)}{n!}$, therefore, $\Delta^n p(x_0)$ is divisible by $n!$. Next, the coefficient of x^{n-1} in p, which is $\frac{\Delta^{n-1} p(x_0)}{(n-1)!}$ plus a multiple of $\frac{\Delta^n p(x_0)}{n!}$, is an integer. But, we have already shown that $\frac{\Delta^n p(x_0)}{n!}$ is an integer, therefore, $\frac{\Delta^{n-1} p(x_0)}{(n-1)!}$ is also an integer. By an inductive proof, we conclude that $\frac{\Delta^m p(x_0)}{m!}$ is an integer for all $m > 0$.

Now, consider the jth term of the Newton's expansion of p around x_0. The expression $(x-x_0)(x-x_0-1)\cdots(x-x_0-j+2)$ is a product of $j-1$ integers, and hence divisible by $(j-1)!$. Since $k!$ divides $(j-1)!$ for all j, such that $k < j \leq n+1$, it is concluded that $k!$ also divides the jth term of the Newton's expansion of p around x_0, for all j such that $k < j \leq n+1$, and the proof of the *if* part of the theorem is complete.

The proof of the *only if* part of the theorem is trivial, as if p is divisible by $k!$ for all integers, then it is divisible by $k!$ for any set of k consecutive integers $\{x_0, x_0 + 1, \cdots, x_0 + k - 1\}$. □

Lemma 3.4.1 indicates that the divisibility by 2 of $p(0)$ and $p(1)$ implies the divisibility by 2 of $p(n)$ for all $n \in \mathbb{Z}$. For example, to decide the divisibility by 2 of $p(n) = n^2 + n$, it suffices to check the divisibility by 2 of just $p(0) = 0$, and $p(1) = 2$. Similarly, the divisibility by 2 of $p(n) = n^{15} + n^{10}$ is implied by the divisibility by 2 of $p(0) = 0$ and $p(1) = 2$.

Given an arbitrary integer m and a polynomial $p(n)$ over $\mathbb{Z}$, $p(n)$ is divisible by m, if and only if $p(n)$ is divisible by m when n assumes a sequence of k consecutive integers, where k is the smallest non-negative integer such that $k!$ is divisible by m. The upper bound of k is $\max_i p_i \cdot n_i$, where $\prod_i p_i^{n_i}$ is the *canonical form* of m. For example, the divisibility by 60 of $p(n)$ is implied by the divisibility by 60 of $p(0), p(1), p(2), p(3)$, and $p(4)$, since 60 divides $5! = 120$. Also, the divisibility by 8 of $p(n)$ is implied by the divisibility by 8 of $p(0), p(1), p(2)$, and $p(3)$, since 8 divides $4! = 24$.

Example **3.4.1** *Prove that $n^5 - n$ is divisible by 30 for all $n \in \mathbb{Z}$.*

PROOF. Since 30 divides $5!$, the divisibility by 30 of $p(n) = n^5 - n$ is implied by the divisibility by 30 of $p(0) = 0$, $p(1) = 0$, $p(2) = 30$, $p(3) = 240$, and $p(4) = 1020$. □

This method is capable of handling complicated multivariate polynomials; however, it is not practical when the integer against which divisibility is tested has large prime factors or large multiplicities. The test can be applied to multivariate polynomials by treating them as univariate polynomials in one of their variables, and apply the test recursively. The choice of the dominant variable does not change the test's conclusion, but may effect the efficiency of the test.

3.5 INTERPRETATION OF FLOW GRAPH NODES

Flow graph nodes are interpreted in the context of the information that reaches them. To avoid the exponential growth of information, we shall interpret each node in an environment which contains the intersection of information of all *live* incoming edges to that node. Thus, before interpretation of a node, all its predecessors in the control flow graph must have been interpreted. This is clearly possible for the acyclic control flow graphs. Strongly connected components of the control flow graph are identified by loop analysis and are treated as single entities. Thus, any control flow graph, cyclic or acyclic, will be viewed as a directed acyclic graph by this hierarchical interpretation. Interpretation of nodes in the context of their predecessors enables the compiler to identify *dead* edges, that is, those edges that the compiler can prove that execution control will never reach. Dead code will be eliminated and will not have any effect on computing the context in which a node is interpreted. Figure 3.5 shows the whole process of interpreting a node of the control flow graph. The transformation T performed by a node is approximated by an operator F, and the effect of F on the incoming information is augmented with the control flow information on the outgoing edges from the node.

If a variable that is used in a node has the same abstract symbolic value on all incoming edges to that node, then the environment in which that node is interpreted will initially bind that variable to its corresponding abstract value. Otherwise, a new abstract value is created for that variable at that point as a result of join of information. The point at which new abstract values are born is called the *birth point* of the abstract values. The *entry* node of a program control flow graph is thus a birth point for all variables that are used in the program. There is another

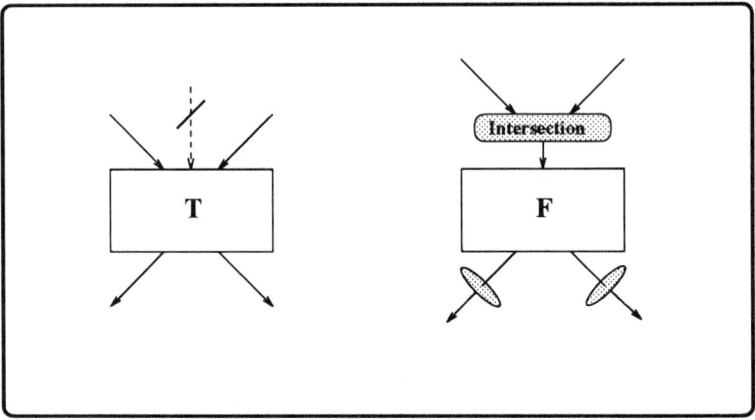

Figure 3.5 Finding the abstract function of a flow graph node.

circumstance under which a new abstract value is created for a variable, and that is the case where a variable is modified as the side effect of an operation that cannot be precisely abstracted. For example, when a value is read for a variable from an input file. To distinguish between different newborn abstract values of the same variable, a new field is added to the abstract value data structure; pointers to the variables in the symbol table are augmented with identification tags that uniquely determine the birth point of the newborn values.

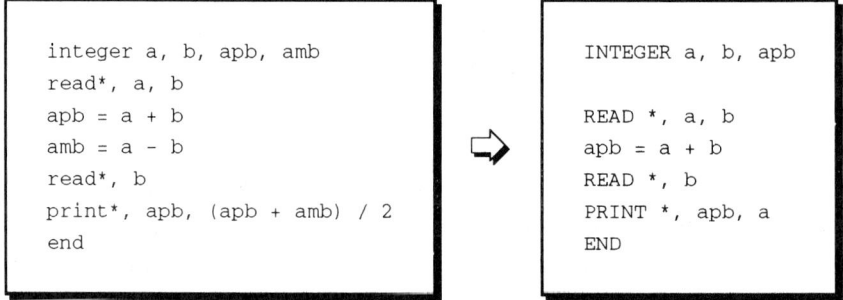

Figure 3.6 Transformation of a code segment by Parafrase-2.

Symbolic information collected by the above method will have the important property that every variable will have just one abstract symbolic

SYMBOLIC ANALYSIS 23

value at any point of the program. Figure 3.6 shows a code segment and its transformed code generated by Parafrase-2. In the *print* statement of the source code, the birth point of the abstract symbolic value of the expressions (apb+amb)/2 and b are the first and the second read statements respectively. Note that substitution of the values of the variables apb and amb in the print statement is not valid in traditional *def-use chains* approach because their definitions are *killed* by the second read statement. However, our abstract interpretation scheme easily discovers that the expression (apb+amb)/2 will always be equal to the value of the variable a at the point where print statement is executed.

3.6 INTERPRETATION OF PROGRAM LOOPS

The power of a parallelizing compiler depends critically on its ability to analyze loops for extraction and exploitation of the available parallelism. Loops may be defined by the dominance relation [ASU86], or by doing a depth first search traversal of the program control flow graph [Hec77]. By loops, we mean *natural loops* as defined by the dominance relation. A natural loop has two essential properties [ASU86]. First, there is a single entry point in the loop, called the *header*, that dominates all nodes in the loop. This means that every path from the initial node of the control flow graph to a node of the loop goes through the loop header. Second, there is at least one path in the loop back to the header. The final edge on such a path is called a *back edge*.

Derivation of the functional behavior of a given program which has a cyclic flow graph is a non-trivial task. Loops might introduce an infinite number of execution paths in a given program. Hence, the effect of program loops should be conservatively approximated in some way in order to be able to derive the symbolic representation of computations of the program for all paths. By careful analysis of the body of a loop, the compiler might be able to discover some patterns in the loop iteration

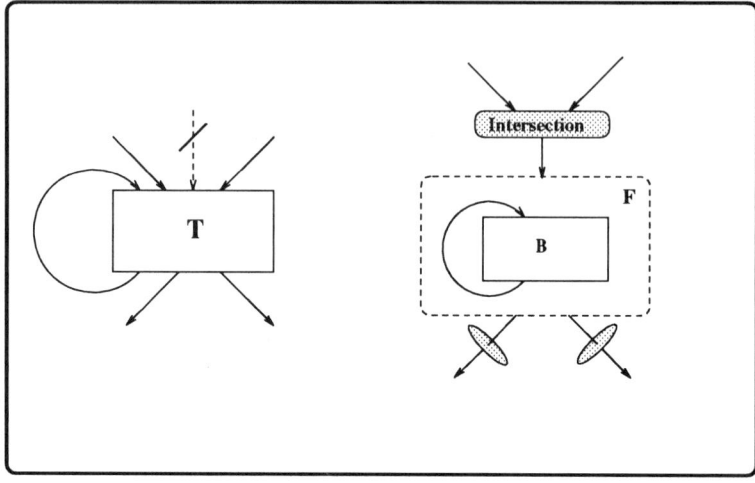

Figure 3.7 Finding the abstract function of a loop.

space from which an abstract model for the loop can be deduced. Using the live loop invariant information that reaches a loop, the abstract model of the loop can be computed by solving the system of recurrence relations that describes the behavior of the loop. By replacing each loop with its abstract model, cyclic control flow graphs are transformed to directed acyclic graphs. In the case of non-reducible control flow graphs, replacing each non-reducible subgraph by its abstract model will make the control flow graphs acyclic. Then, the compiler can try to solve the loop exit conditions symbolically to find the net effect of the execution of the whole loop on the program variables. In other words, each loop is modeled by an abstract operator that maps an input environment to an output one. Live loop invariant information that reaches a loop is used in the analysis of the loop body as shown in Figure 3.7.

3.6.1 Nesting of Loops

It can be shown that when two natural loops have different headers, they are either disjoint or one is entirely contained (*nested*) within the other [ASU86]. However, when two natural loops have the same header, the loop nesting is ambiguous. In such cases, structure normalization can be used to transform the loops in such a way that each loop is uniquely identified by its header. Note that the resulting loop nesting, grounded upon natural loops, might be different from that determined by other definitions of loops, such as those based on *interval analysis* [All70, Coc70], *T1-T2 analysis* [Ull73], and *control dependence analysis* [FOW87]. Wolfe [Wol90]has studied the implication of various definitions of loops on loop nesting.

Making loops uniquely identifiable by their headers results in a simpler scheme for interpretation of loops. Parafrase-2 normalizes the structure of loops of the following categories. In each case, data flow information, including the dominance relation, is incrementally updated at the required points.

1. Loops that are not contained in each other and are not disjoint - such loops are combined together by creating a new node and having all the back edges go to the new node instead of the header. A single back edge goes from the new node to the header. Figure 3.8shows this transformation together with induction variable substitution, performed by Parafrase-2. Fixed *do*loops that have *if terminators*belong to this category [CFS90, HP92].

2. Loops that are contained in each other and share the loop header - in such cases it is natural to assume that the loop that is contained in another one is nested within it (although from the point of view of frequency of execution, it could be the other way). A new header is created for the outer loop, and its back edge is also changed accordingly. Figure 3.9shows this transformation, performed by Parafrase-2.

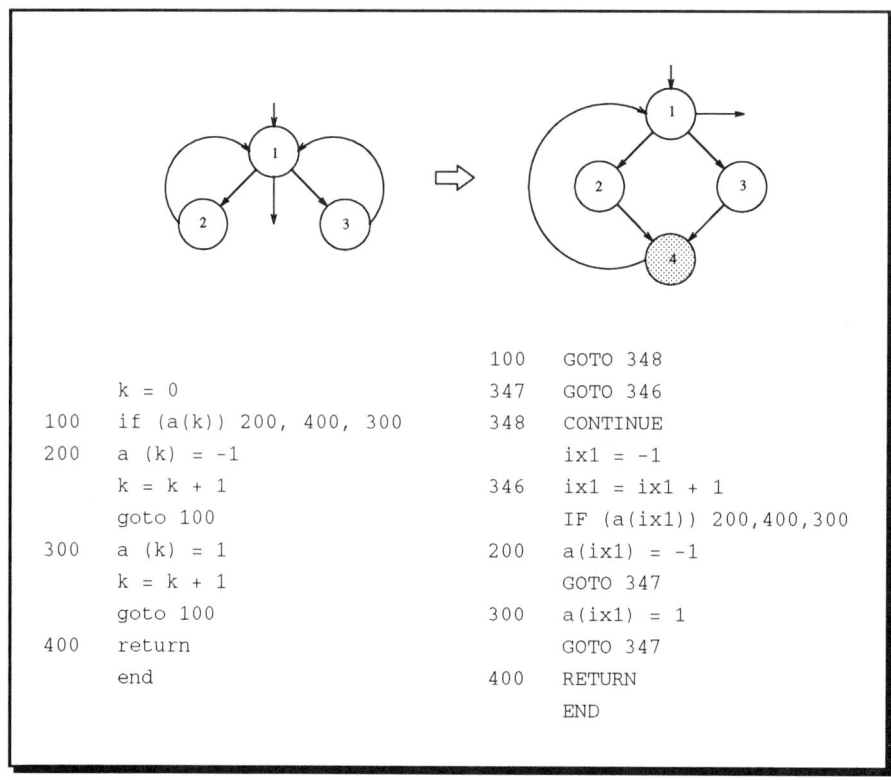

Figure 3.8 Non-nested, non-disjoint loops are merged together.

SYMBOLIC ANALYSIS

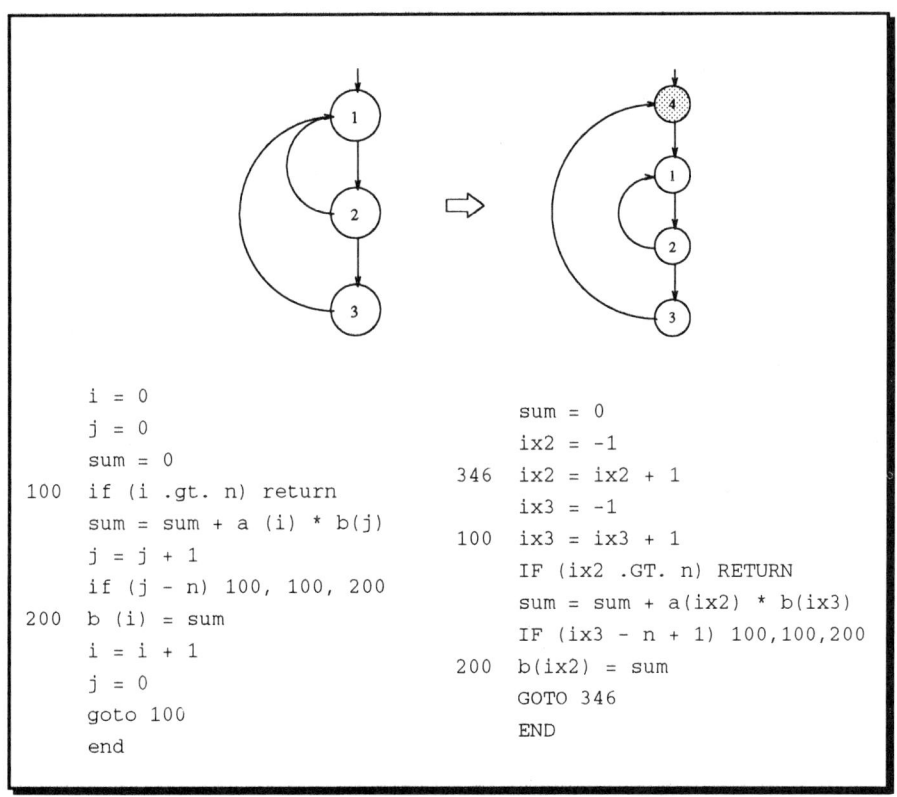

Figure 3.9 Normalization of nested loops that share header.

3.6.2 Loop Analysis

Loop analysis should provide information about values of program variables at different iterations of the loop and also the net effect of execution of the loop on the variables. To achieve the former goal, the closed form of expressions inside the loop should be found. Knowledge about number of iterations of the loop is required for finding the net effect of the execution of the loop.

The basic strategy for finding the closed form of expressions inside a loop is as follows. Each variable that might be referenced inside the loop is assigned a symbolic value. Then the loop body in an arbitrary iteration is interpreted in the abstract symbolic domain, introduced in the previous sections. This is accomplished by trying to interpret the node that corresponds to the head of the loop back edge, which in turn will result in the interpretation of the whole loop body. The result of this interpretation will be a system of recurrence relations for the expressions inside the loop. The solution to the system of recurrence relations would give the value of expressions at different iterations as a function of the loop index variable and initial values of variables that reach the loop. For nested loops, the process is applied recursively, starting from the innermost loop.

```
if (n .gt. 0) then
    y = 0
    do j = 1, n
        x = y + a
        y = x + b
    end do
    print*, y
end if
```

⇨

```
IF (n .GT. 0) THEN
    y = 0
    DO j = 1,n
        x = a * j - b + b * j
        y = a * j + b * j
    END DO
    PRINT *, a * n + b * n
END IF
```

Figure 3.10 Loop analysis in a case with cyclic dependences.

SYMBOLIC ANALYSIS

Obtaining the solutions to the recurrence relations is not always a straightforward task. Complications arise in cases of simultaneous recurrences, where several variables that are dependent on each other are modified in a loop. In particular, interdependences between different recurrences might be cyclic ; x may depend on y, which depends on x.

Due to its importance in complexity analysis of algorithms, automatic solution of difference equations has been the subject of several studies [CK77b, GJ78, Ivi78, Kar81]. Parafrase-2 uses the method of finite differences to solve the system of recurrence relations obtained by symbolic interpretation of loops. Our experimental results indicate that this simple technique is powerful enough for handling the most complicated cases of recurrences that arise in the analysis of computation of array subscripts inside loops in real benchmark programs. This method, which has enabled our compiler to solve cases with cyclic interdependences, will be discussed in detail in Chapter 4. Figure 3.10 shows the result of loop analysis, performed by Parafrase-2, in a case with cyclic flow dependences. Note that the recurrence relations that describe the behavior of the loop in this case are not cyclic. However, the loop shown in Figure 3.11 is a case where recurrence relations with cyclic interdependences are involved. The result of loop analysis and dead code elimination, performed by Parafrase-2, is also shown in the same figure.

After substitution of induction expressions of a loop is done, the compiler tries to find out the number of iterations of the loop. If the loop exit condition contains only occurrences of loop index variable and loop invariant variables, then the compiler looks for solutions to the loop exit condition. The smallest non-negative value of the loop index variable that satisfies the loop exit condition is the number of iterations of the loop. Note that at this point the compiler may need to verify a constraint among some of the program variables, that is the existence of a non-negative solution to the loop exit equation. The problem of finding the solution to the loop exit equation, and even the question of existence of such a solution, in the general case, is clearly undecidable,

```
implicit integer (a-z)
read*, n
if (n .gt. 0) then
    x = 1
    y = 2
    do j = 1, 2*n
        t = x
        x = y
        y = t
        print*, x
        print*, y
    end do
    print*, x, y
end if
end
```

```
INTEGER n, j

READ *, n
IF (n .GT. 0) THEN
    DO j = 1,2*n
        PRINT *, ((-1)**(j-1)+3)/2
        PRINT *, ((-1)**j+3)/2
    END DO
    PRINT *, 1, 2
END IF
END
```

Figure 3.11 A loop with cyclic recurrence relations.

as implied by unsolvability of the halting problem. In fact, the problem remains undecidable, even if the loop exit equation is restricted to be a polynomial in the loop index variable, of arbitrary degree, with constant integer coefficients. This is shown in the following theorem.

```
n = 0
DO WHILE (p(n) .ne. 0)
    n = n + 1
END DO
```

Figure 3.12 Unsolvability of the loop termination problem.

THEOREM **3.6.1** *The problem of deciding termination of execution of program loops is undecidable even if the loop exit conditions are restricted to be tests of equality of polynomials of loop index variables.*

SYMBOLIC ANALYSIS

PROOF. This theorem is a trivial consequence of the Matijasevič's result on the unsolvability of the *Hilbert's Tenth Problem* [DMR76, JM91, Mat93], and can be proved as follows. Consider the loop shown in Figure 3.12, and assume that p, the condition of the loop, is an integer-valued polynomial of arbitrary degree in n. Observe that the loop enumerates non-negative integers starting from zero until a non-negative integer n is found that satisfies $p(n) = 0$. If such an n exists then the loop terminates, otherwise the loop runs forever. In other words, the loop will terminate if and only if the diophantine equation $p(x) = 0$ has a non-negative solution. But, Matijasevičhas shown that it is not possible to devise an algorithm to decide whether an arbitrary diophantine equation has a solution in natural numbers. Hence, we conclude that it is not possible to count the number of iterations of program loops even when the exit conditions of the loops are restricted to be polynomials of arbitrary degree in loop index variables. □

```
            a = 0
            b = 0
            y = 0
    100     if (y.gt.x) goto 200
            y = y+3*a+3*b+1
            a = a+2*b+1
            b = b+1
            goto 100
    200     print*, b
```

⇒

```
            b = 0
            ix1 = -1
    100     ix1 = ix1+1
            IF ((ix1**3).GT.x) GOTO 200
            b = ix1+1
            GOTO 100
    200     PRINT *, b
```

Figure 3.13 Example of analysis of loop termination by Parafrase-2.

In some cases, however, the simplified loop exit equation can be solved symbolically, and the method of constraint propagation [CH78, HP91]may be used to verify the existence of a non-negative solution. For example, consider the source code shown in Figure 3.13. This program is given in [AO91], in studying complications raised in the verification of programs with loops, as an example of a simple loop that is difficult to understand. The program computes, in a very primitive fashion, the integer cubic root of x, $b = \lfloor \sqrt[3]{x} \rfloor$, given that $x \geq 0$. The transformed code demonstrates that Parafrase-2 has been able to derive and simplify the loop exit condition, as a function of loop invariants and the loop index variable. Note that the loop exit equation can be solved in this case.

```
       s = 0
       do j = 1, n
          s = s + j
          if (cond) goto 99
       end do
       print*, s
       return
99     print*, s
```

⇨

```
       S = 0
       DO j = 1,n
          S = (j + j * j) / 2
          IF (cond) GOTO 99
       END DO
       PRINT *, (n + n * n) / 2
       RETURN
99     PRINT *, S
```

Figure 3.14 Analysis of a loop with multiple exits.

A typical example of a loop is a fixed *do* loop with the start value of 1 and the stop value of n, where n is a program variable that does not change within the loop. In this case, n will be the only solution to the loop exit condition. If the compiler knows that n has a positive value whenever control reaches the *do* statement, then it is correct to assume that n iterations of the loop will be executed. If n could be a non-positive number, then the loop would not execute at all (in older versions of Fortran, the first iteration of the loop would be executed regardless of the loop condition). Hence, if the compiler does not have any information about the positivity of the variable n, then it will use $\max(n, 0)$ as the number of iterations of the loop. This complicates the simplification of expressions that use the final value of the induction variables. This problem, called *zero-trip loop problem* [EHLP91], can cause problems in the analysis of nested loops, and will be addressed in Section 6.3.1.

Figure 3.14 shows the result of loop analysis and induction expression substitution, performed by Parafrase-2, in the case of a loop with

SYMBOLIC ANALYSIS   33

multiple exits. Note that the final value of the induction variable s is known when the loop is completely executed, and not known when the exit from the loop has been taken through the if statement.

```
k = k0
do i = 1, n
   do j = 1, k
      k = k + 1
      a (i, j) = k
   end do
end do
```

⇨

```
CDOALL i = 1,n
   CDOALL j = 1,k0 * 2 ** (i - 1)
      a(i,j) = j + (k0 * 2 ** (i - 1))
   END DO
END DO
```

Figure 3.15 Loop bounds may be modified within the loop.

In Fortran fixed *do* loops, the values of loop index variables' *initial, final*, and *stride* expressions are the values of those expressions computed right before starting the *do* statements. Hence, in cases where the variables that are elements of the symbolic values of these expressions are modified within the loop, the initial values of those variables must be used in the computation of induction expressions. Figure 3.15 shows a Fortran code segment with a nest of fixed *do* loops, in which a variable that represents the final value of the inner loop index variable is modified within the loop. Note that Parafrase-2 has been able to parallelize the loops by deriving the bounds of the inner loop, and by eliminating the extraneous dependence introduced by the definition of the induction variable k. This scheme of induction variable recognition is a fundamental component of our symbolic analysis framework. It is discussed in more details in Chapter 4.

4
INDUCTION VARIABLES

Induction variables are of particular interest in optimizing compilers [ASU86]; a subclass of them that form arithmetic progressions has a vital role in parallelizing compilers [AK87, KKLW80, Wol78]. Induction variables are usually introduced to improve program performance on sequential computers. To illustrate this, we consider the loop of Figure 4.1.

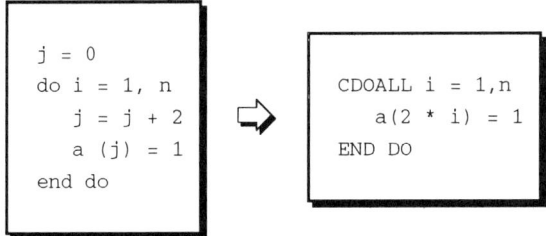

Figure 4.1 Example of linear induction variable substitution.

In the original code, the subscript j of array a assumes a sequence of values described by the arithmetic progression $2, 4, \ldots, 2n$. Variable j is called an *induction variable* of the loop, and its occurrence as the subscript of array a can be replaced by 2*i, where i is the loop index variable. However, the original code has an advantage over the transformed code in that at each iteration of the loop, an addition operation is performed, compared to the more expensive operation of multiplication in the subscript of a(2*i). Furthermore, if there were other occurrences of j in statements of the loop, for each such a reference there would be a multiplication operation in the transformed code, compared to just a simple reference to the variable j in the original code. Replacement of expensive instructions by fast operations is called *strength reduction*, and has been extensively studied for optimizing compilers [ASU86, ACK81, CK77a, FU76, Pai81, PS77]. The classical method of strength reduction is based on the recognition of induction variables.

Computation via strength reduction is an inherently sequential procedure and is not suitable for parallel machines. For instance, in the original code of the above example, the assignment statement that increments the variable j introduces dependences between different iterations of the loop, and prevents parallelization of the loop. On the other hand, by substituting the closed form of the induction variable j for its occurrence as the subscript of array a, the increment statement becomes useless and can be eliminated from the loop. Thus, no dependences remain between iterations of the loop, and it can run in parallel. The above transformation, called *induction variable substitution*, is the inverse of strength reduction and has been used in parallelizing compilers for a number of years [PW86]. By this transformation, every occurrence of an induction variable is replaced by a linear function of its enclosing loop index variables.

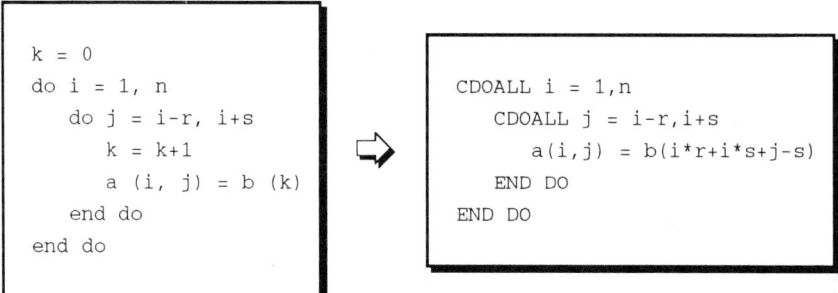

Figure 4.2   Linear induction variables in trapezoidal loops.

INDUCTION VARIABLES

4.1 GENERALIZED INDUCTION VARIABLES

In experiments with Perfect Benchmarks® (programs TRFD and OCEAN), variables similar to induction variables have been found for which there exist closed forms that are not linear in the enclosing loop index variables. They have been named *Generalized Induction Variables* or *GIVs* [AHI90, EHJ+91, EHLP91, HP92, Wol92]. The sequence of values that a GIV receives throughout the execution of a loop does not necessarily form an arithmetic progression. A set of program constructs that may produce such GIVs are triangular and trapezoidal loops, which generate GIVs that can be characterized by polynomials in terms of enclosing loop index variables. None of the state-of-the-art parallelizing compilers[1] that we studied could handle these cases, surprisingly not even when the loop bounds were in such a way that they resulted in linear induction variables. An example of a trapezoidal loop with a linear induction variable, together with its transformed code generated by Parafrase-2, is shown in Figure 4.2.

Another program pattern that may result in GIVs is the geometric progression that produces GIVs that can be described by exponential functions in terms of the corresponding loop index variables. Figure 4.3 is an example of GIVs generated by triangular loops and geometric progression.

Structure of loops in scientific application programs is sometimes more complex than that of the above examples, and thus can result in much more complicated GIVs. The code segment of Figure 4.4 is extracted from program TRFD in Perfect Benchmarks®. Figure 4.5 shows its transformed version generated by Parafrase-2. In fact, the original code in TRFD is even more complicated than that shown here. It requires a precise wraparound variable analysis that is discussed in Section 4.5. To our knowledge, Parafrase-2 is the only existing parallelizing compiler capable of handling the actual case. Elimination

---
[1] See Table 7.1 in Chapter 7.

```
k = 0
do i = 1, m
    do j = 1, i
        k = k + 1
        a (i, j) = b (k)
    end do
end do
j = 1
k = 1
id = ix - iy
do i = 1, n
    j = j * ix + j * iy
    t (i) = j
    k = k * id
    z (i) = k
end do
```

```
CDOALL i = 1, m
    CDOALL j = 1, i
        a(i,j) = b((-i+i*i+2*j)/2)
    END DO
END DO
CDOALL i = 1, n
    t(i) = (ix+iy)**i
    z(i) = (ix-iy)**i
END DO
```

Figure 4.3   Parafrase-2 recognizes generalized induction variables.

of the dependences introduced by the assignments to the variable mijkl requires a sophisticated symbolic analysis and global forward substitution scheme. In particular, derivation of the closed form of the induction variable mijkl in terms of variables mor b and num, which is necessary for dependence analysis, requires the capability of symbolic division that was addressed in Section 3.3. Parafrase-2 is able to handle even more complicated cases where the loop bounds are not necessarily linear expressions of enclosing loop index variables, but rather polynomials of arbitrary degrees in terms of the enclosing loop index variables and invariants [HP92].

The code segment shown in Figure 4.4 account for 29% of the overall execution time of the program TRFD. Its parallelization requires recognition of generalized induction variables, and results in a loop speedup of 12.3 on the Cedar multiprocessor [EHLP91]. The most important loop of the program TRFD accounts for 69% of its overall execution

INDUCTION VARIABLES

```
nrs = (num * (num + 1)) / 2
nij = (morb * (morb + 1)) / 2
mijkl = 0
mij = 0
mleft = nrs - nij
do mi = 1, morb
   do mj = 1, mi
      mij = mij + 1
      mijkl = mijkl + mi - mj + 1
      do mk = mi + 1, morb
         do ml = 1, mk
            mijkl = mijkl + 1
            xijkl (mijkl) = xkl (ml)
         end do
      end do
      mijkl = mijkl + mij + mleft
   end do
end do
```

Figure 4.4 A code segment extracted from program TRFD.

```
DO mi = 1, morb
   DO mj = 1, mi
      DO mk = mi + 1, morb
         DO ml = 1, mk
            xijkl((mi * mi * num + mi * mi * num * num -
            mi * num - mi * num * num + 2 * mj * num +
            2 * mj * num * num - 2 * mk + 2 * mk * mk +
            4 * ml - 2 * num - 2 * num * num) / 4) = xkl (ml)
         END DO
      END DO
   END DO
END DO
```

Figure 4.5 Induction analysis of the code segment of Figure 4.4.

time. Also, parallelization of that loop requires capability of handling non-linear induction variables, and results in a loop speedup of 16.4 on the Cedar multiprocessor [EHLP91]. In the program OCEAN, one loop that performs 40% of the operations of the whole program could be parallelized after recognition and substitution of the corresponding generalized induction variable. This results in a speedup of 8.1 on the Cedar multiprocessor [EHJ+91].

4.2 GENERALIZED INDUCTION EXPRESSIONS

The notion of GIVs can be further generalized to what we call *Generalized Induction Expressions*. This generalization is based on the observation that it is possible to have some of the expressions of a loop described by closed formulas, while none of the program variables at the source level are induction variables. This generalization is independent of the definition of induction variables. In other words, regardless of how inclusive the definition of induction variables is, some variables may assume values that make it impossible for the compiler to derive their closed forms, while the closed forms of particular functions of those variables might be derivable by the compiler. Expression $j +k$ in Figure 4.6 is such a case detected by Parafrase-2. Note that in this example, none of the occurrences of the variables j and k inside the loop can be described by a closed form in terms of a loop index variable and invariants.

We define a *generalized induction expression* ε of a loop $\mathcal{L}$ to be an expression appearing in a statement of the loop $\mathcal{L}$, where the sequence of values that ε assumes at different iterations of $\mathcal{L}$ can be described by a function χ, of the form $\chi(n) = \varphi(n) + ar^n$, where n is an integer variable which identifies the loop iteration number, φ is an integer-valued polynomial of finite degree in n whose coefficients are loop-invariant expressions, and a and r are loop-invariant expressions. In such a case, χ is called the *characteristic function* of the induction

INDUCTION VARIABLES

```
100  n = irandom (iseed)
     j = j + n + 1
     k = k - n
     print*, j, k
     print*, j + k
     if (cond) goto 100
```

⇨

```
     j0 = j
     k0 = k
     ix1 = -1
100  ix1 = ix1 + 1
     n = irandom(iseed)
     j = j + n + 1
     k = k - n
     PRINT *, j, k
     PRINT *, ix1 + j0 + k0 + 1
     IF (cond) GOTO 100
```

Figure 4.6 An induction expression recognized by Parafrase-2.

expression ε. The following theorem shows the undecidability of the induction expression problem.

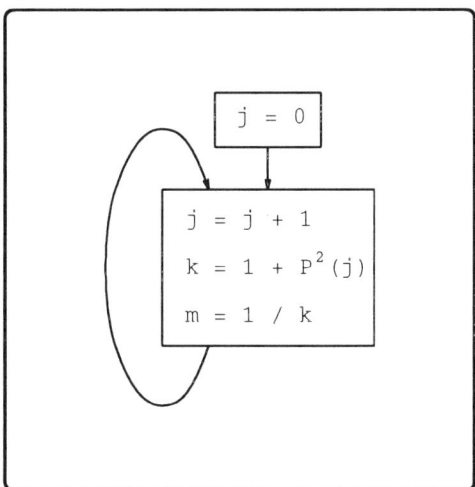

Figure 4.7 Undecidability of the induction expression problem.

THEOREM **4.2.1** *It is not possible to devise an algorithm that would decide whether an expression of an arbitrary loop is an induction expression of a given degree.*

PROOF. We show that existence of such an algorithm contradicts a known fact. Consider the loop of Figure 4.7, in which P is an arbitrary polynomial with integer coefficients, and the division operation of the last assignment statement is of integer type. If we had an algorithm that could decide whether an expression of an arbitrary loop is an induction expression of a given degree, then we would be able to decide whether m will be constant in all iterations or not. That is, we could decide whether $1/k$ is an induction expression of degree zero or not.

Note that variable j in the given loop enumerates all non-negative integers in ascending order. If the general diophantine equation $P(x) = 0$ has no roots in natural numbers, then $P(j) \neq 0, \forall j \in \mathbb{N}$, $P^2(j) > 0, \forall j \in \mathbb{N}$, $k = P^2(j) + 1 > 1, \forall j \in \mathbb{N}$, and consequently $1/k$ will be equal to zero. Conversely, if $1/k$ is zero in all iterations of the loop, then $|k| > 1$, given that k is always a positive integer, we conclude that $k > 1$, and hence $P^2(j) > 0, \forall j \in \mathbb{N}$, which implies that $P(j) \neq 0, \forall j \in \mathbb{N}$. Therefore, the diophantine equation $P(x) = 0$ has no roots in natural numbers if and only if $1/k$ is an induction expression of the loop, or put it another way, the diophantine equation $P(x) = 0$ has a root in natural numbers if and only if $1/k$ is not an induction expression of the loop.

Have we had a procedure that could decide whether an expression of an arbitrary loop is an induction expression of a given degree, we would be able to devise an algorithm that could decide whether an arbitrary diopahntine equation has a root in natural numbers. Matijasevičhas shown that such an algorithm does not exist [DMR76, JM91, Mat93]. □

An induction variable of a loop may have different characteristic functions at different points of the loop. This case, usually a result of coupled induction variables, or multiple assignments to the same induction variable in a loop nest, is especially important from a practical point of view, as it occurs so often in real programs. In our study on Perfect Benchmarks®, we observed this case in the programs ADM, MDG, MG3D, and SPEC77. Automatic analysis of these cases requires

INDUCTION VARIABLES 43

a precise symbolic analysis, and was missing from the parallelizing compilers that we studied (See Table 7.1 in Chapter 7). Parafrase-2 could handle all those cases automatically and without any user assertions.

```
ik = 1
jiz = 2
do i = 1, norder
    do k = 1, natmo3
        ji = jiz
        ikl = ik + natmo3
        s = 0.0d0
        do l = i, norder
            s = s + c(ji) * v(ikl)
            ikl = ikl + natmo3
            ji = ji + 1
        end do
        v(ik) = v(ik) + s
        ik = ik + 1
    end do
    jiz = jiz + norder + 1
end do
```

⇨

```
DO i = 1, norder
    DO k = 1, natmo3
        s = 0.0d0
        DO l = i, norder
            s = s +
                c(i*norder+l-norder+1)
                *v(k+l*natmo3)
        END DO
        v(i*natmo3+k-natmo3) =
            v(i*natmo3+k-natmo3)+s
    END DO
END DO
```

Figure 4.8 Induction analysis of a code segment of MDG.

In their empirical investigation of the effectiveness and limitations of automatic parallelization [SH92], Singh and Hennessy find the need for a *fairly sophisticated induction variable analysis* to be able to parallelize the middle loop of the source program shown in Figure 4.8. This code is the prediction phase of the predictor-corrector method used in program MDG: an N-body molecular dynamics simulation. As is evident from Figure 4.8 Parafrase-2 has successfully derived closed forms of all of the induction variables of this code. This example shows the superiority of our unified approach to semantic analysis over schemes based on the repetitive application of induction variable analysis and forward substitution in an ad hoc manner. Ad hoc approaches will be more expensive and less effective in this case.

The source code shown in Figure 4.9 is a loop nest extracted from subroutine FFS99 of program SPEC77 in Perfect Benchmarks®. The structure of computations in these loops is such that all loops can run in parallel. Detection of parallelism in this simple case requires a precise induction variable recognition and forward substitution scheme. We tried this loop nest on KAP. It could not discover the parallelism in any of the loops, not even the inner loops. The reason is the inability of handling coupled induction variables with multiple characteristic functions. To parallelize the inner loops, the compiler needs to know the relation between the initial value of the variables `i` and `j` before the execution of the inner loops. These variables are modified not only in the outer loops but also in inner loops. Furthermore, parallelization of the second loop nest requires information about last values assigned to the variables `ibase` and `jbase`.

The structure of the most important loops of subroutines FFS99 and FFA99 in SPEC77 is similar to that shown in Figure 4.9, and global propagation of information is essential for parallelization of this code. These subroutines are important components of the whole program, as they are called several times within main loops. In fact, one of the reasons for the poor performance of parallelizing compilers on program SPEC77 is the perceived, but nonexistent, data dependences as a result of compilers limitations on handling coupled induction variables with multiple assignments [Blu92]. Derivation of induction variables in these subroutines would further help in identifying the range of array accesses, proving privatizability of array `a`, and parallelizing the caller loops. Subroutines CPASS, CPASSM, RPASS, and RPASSM from the program MG3D have also loops with similar structure. They require an even more precise analysis, because the number of symbolic parameters that are involved is larger than shown here. Nevertheless, our symbolic analyzer handles all of them.

The output of symbolic analyzer of Parafrase-2 on the source loop nest of Figure 4.9 was given to KAP as input. KAP parallelized the outer loops and vectorized the inner loops, without any additional sophistication for

INDUCTION VARIABLES 45

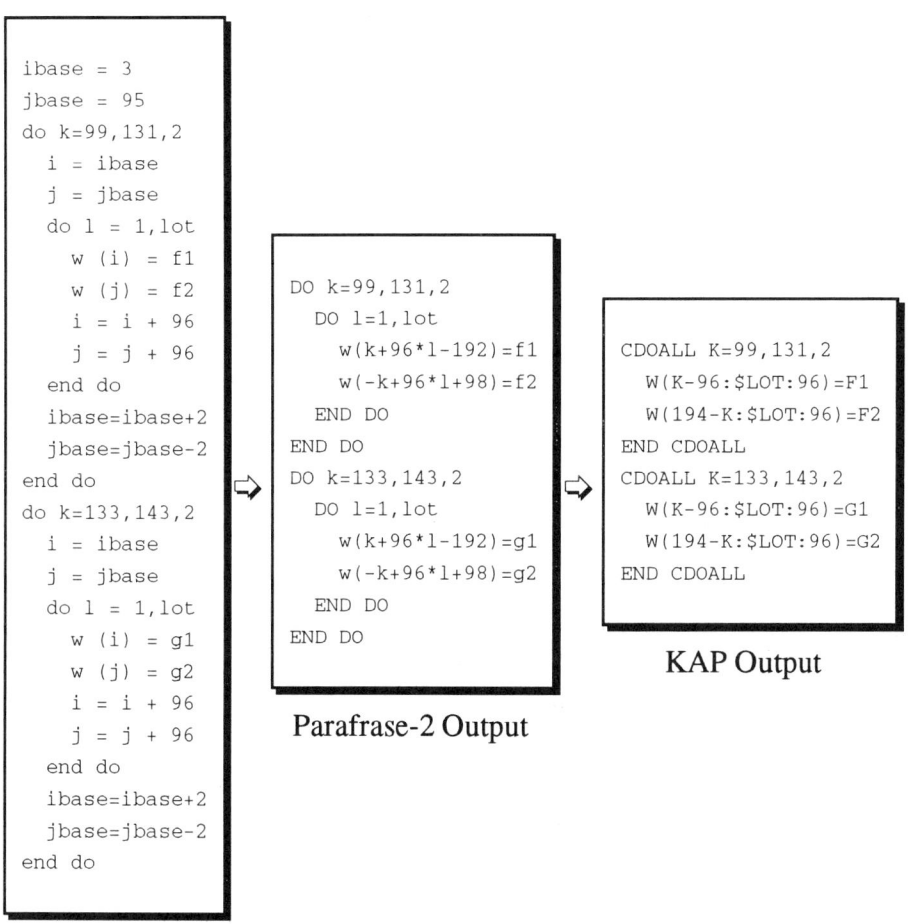

Figure 4.9 Parallelization of a code segment of SPEC77.

dependence analysis. Basically, symbolic analysis of Parafrase-2 had resolved all the ambiguities for dependence analysis. From the other parallelizing compilers that we tried (See Table 7.1 in Chapter 7), Titan was the only one that could partially solve the problem; it parallelized just the first loop. It could not parallelize the second loop because of its inability in global propagation of information.

4.3 SYMBOLIC INTERPOLATION

The problem of induction expression recognition and substitution can be considered as a special case of symbolic interpolation in which the form of interpolating function is restricted based on the definition of induction expressions. Consider the case of an induction expression ε characterized by the function $\chi(n) = \varphi(n) + ar^n$, where n identifies the loop iteration number, φ is an integer-valued polynomial in n of degree m with loop-invariant coefficients, and a and r are loop-invariant expressions. Let the *forward difference operator* Δ be defined by $\Delta\chi(n) = \chi(n+1) - \chi(n)$. Each term in the successive differences of φ is the sum of two parts, one arising from $\varphi(n)$, and the other from ar^n. Since $\varphi(n)$ is a polynomial of degree m, the part arising from it will vanish after $m + 1$ differences, and the remaining parts in differences will form a geometric progression with the common ratio r.

Conversely, if the first few terms of a series are known, and if the mth differences of these terms form a geometric progression whose common ratio is r, then we may assume that the general term of the given series is of the form $\varphi(n) + ar^n$, where φ is an integer-valued polynomial in n of degree $m - 1$. This suggests an algorithm for recognition and substitution of generalized induction expressions. Given a loop, the compiler can execute a few iterations of the loop body symbolically, and save the symbolic value of each expression at each iteration. The more iterations executed, the higher degree interpolating polynomials can be discovered.

INDUCTION VARIABLES

By executing two iterations of the loop symbolically, loop-invariant expressions can be recognized. Linear induction expressions can be found by executing at most three iterations of the loop symbolically. In fact, just two iterations are enough for recognition of linear induction variables whose differences in two successive iterations are scalar constants. The extra iteration is necessary to recognize linear induction variables whose differences in two successive iterations are loop invariant expressions, but not scalar constants. In general, induction expressions of degree m can be recognized by executing at most $m + 2$ iterations of the loop symbolically [2].

Parafrase-2 allows the user to specify the highest degree of interpolating polynomials that the compiler should find. This provides a dynamic control of the tradeoff between compilation time and the accuracy of compilation analysis, and enables the compiler to use a higher degree of precision when analyzing an important loop of a program. After finding the symbolic value of expressions, the compiler builds up the difference table, and using the Newton's Forward Formula for interpolation, stated below, it derives the interpolating functions. Note that in many cases the whole difference table need not be constructed, and by appropriate order of computation, extraneous calculation can be avoided.

4.3.1 Newton's Forward Formula for Interpolation

Suppose that the value of function f at the equally spaced points $x_0, x_1, \ldots, x_n$ is known, and suppose that $\Delta^{n+1} f = 0$. Assuming $h = x_i - x_{i-1}, \forall i, 1 \leq i \leq n$, the polynomial p, interpolating f at $x_0, x_1, \ldots, x_n$, is given by $p(x) = \sum_{i=0}^{n} \Delta^i f(x_0) \binom{r}{i}$, where $r = (x - x_0)/h$ [Jor65].

---

[2] The maximum m needed to handle all loops of the Perfect Benchmarks® is three, and most of the induction variables of real codes can be recognized by executing two iterations of the loops symbolically.

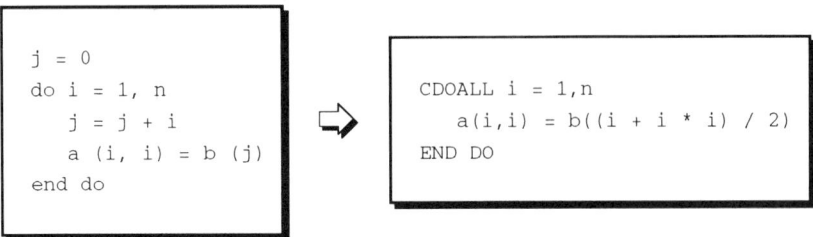

Figure 4.10 Example of a nonlinear induction variable.

To illustrate the above method, consider the source program of Figure 4.10. Let the symbolic value of the variable j at the beginning of the ith iteration of the loop be denoted by j. The expression j+i will assume the values $j+i, j+2i+1, j+3i+3$ at iterations $i, i+1, i+2$ respectively. Figure 4.11 illustrates the computation of the difference table for the expression j+i. Since the second difference of the given values is a constant, the compiler recognizes j+i as a quadratic induction expression. Assuming i represents the loop iteration number, and i_0 and j_0 are symbolic values of the variables i and j at the beginning of the first iteration of the loop, by using the Newton's Forward Formula for the interpolating polynomial, the compiler comes up with the following polynomial for the expression j+i:

$$\chi(i) = j_0 + i_0 + (i_0 + 1)\binom{i-1}{1} + \binom{i-1}{2}.$$

Using the reaching flow information to the loop header, the compiler discovers the facts that $i_0 = 1$, and $j_0 = 0$. By substituting these values in the above formula, the characteristic function of the induction expression j+i is derived as $\chi(i) = \frac{i+i^2}{2}$.

The final value of variable j after execution of the loop will be $(n+n^2)/2$, provided that variable n is non-negative. This value will be propagated to the loop successor. Note that correctness of this propagation critically depends on the execution of the loop. If the variable n has a negative value, the loop will not execute at all, and the final value of variable j

INDUCTION VARIABLES

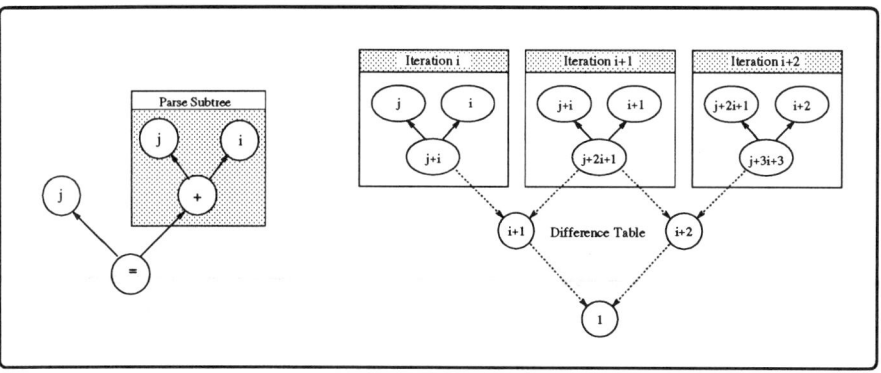

Figure 4.11 Symbolic Computation Tree of an expression.

will be 0, and not $(n+n^2)/2$. In fact, the final value of variable j can be described by the closed form $(\max(n,0) + \max^2(n,0))/2$ for all values of n.

The problem of determining the number of iterations of a loop is of great importance in handling multiply nested loops. The technique of constraint propagation [CH78, HP91] can often be used to prove the execution of loops for at least one iteration, and thus avoid the complications that arise from having max and min functions in the expressions. In the cases where this cannot be proved, algebraic techniques developed in Section 6.3.1 can be used for the derivation and simplification of characteristic functions and the final values of induction variables.

4.4 INDUCTION EXPRESSIONS WITH CONDITIONAL STATEMENTS

Most of the parallelizing/optimizing compilers do not recognize the induction variables that are target of assignment statements under the control of conditional statements. Parafrase-2 recognizes such cases of induction expressions, and derives their characteristic functions. In these cases, induction expressions can be abstracted by a single function, regardless of the executed path, and regardless of the way the elements that form these expressions have been computed. Figure 4.12 shows the result of induction expression analysis and dead code elimination performed by Parafrase-2 in a case where an induction variable is assigned under conditional statements in a nested loop. None of the state-of-the-art parallelizing compilers (See Table 7.1 in Chapter 7) that we tested could handle this case.

```
k = 0
do i = 1, n
    if (cond (i)) then
        do j = 1, i
            k = k + j
            a (i, j) = b (k)
        end do
    else
        k = k+(i*(i+1))/2
    end if
end do
```

⇨

```
CDOALL i = 1,n
    IF (cond(i)) THEN
        CDOALL j = 1,i
            a(i,j)=b((-i+i**3+3*j+3*j*j)/6)
        END DO
    ELSE
    END IF
END DO
```

Figure 4.12 Parafrase-2 recognizes conditional induction variables.

4.5 WRAPAROUND EXPRESSIONS

Traditionally, wraparound variables of order n of a loop are defined to be those variables that are not induction variables of the loop, but will become induction variables when the first n iterations are peeled off the loop [Lea85, PW86, Wol92]. Typically, wraparound variables are of order one. For instance, this may occur when in a loop a variable is used before it is defined in terms of the loop index variable. The standard trick is to peel off the first iteration of the loop, and replace the wraparound variable with the appropriate induction variable [Wol92]. Wraparound variables have been given special consideration by researchers and commercial compilers [Kuc88, Lea85]because they appear often in real application programs. In our experiments with Perfect Benchmarks®, we observed occurrences of wraparound variables in programs TRFD and ADM.

It is interesting to note that our definition of generalized induction variables is inclusive enough to contain wraparound variables of first order as special cases of induction variables. In fact, any wraparound expression of first order, as defined by the traditional definition, is a generalized expression where the base of the exponential part of its characteristic function is zero. In particular, our symbolic analyzer discovers cases of wraparound expressions in which the value of the expressions at the first iteration turns out to match the pattern of the sequence of values they assume starting from the second iteration.

For example, consider the source code shown in Figure 4.13together with its code transformed by the symbolic analyzer of Parafrase-2. Both j and kare wraparound variables in the traditional sense, but the value of j, as the subscript expression of array a at the first iteration of the loop, matches the closed formula which is found for the remaining iterations. This point has also been observed by Wolfe [Wol92]. On the other hand, the value of kat the first iteration is not known, but the symbolic analyzer of Parafrase-2 has been able to derive a formula that covers all iterations of the loop. Note that the whole exponential part of the characteristic function of k will be zero in all iterations except the first one. No special case analysis has been done to cast this case as an induction variable. Recognition of this particular class of induction variables is a result of our abstract interpreter knowledge that in the domain of integers, 0^n is equal to zero when n is positive, is equal to one for n equal to zero, and is undefined when n is negative.

It should be noted that 0^0 is one of the indeterminate forms in analysis, but is defined to be one in axiomatic number theory [Eis71]. All the computers that we are aware of evaluate the integer expression 0^0 to one. Knuth [Knu92] surveys the history of the mathematical debate on whether 0^0 should be defined as one or *undefined*, and mentions several cases related to integers in which it is desirable to have 0^0 defined as one. Whether or not 0^0 is defined as one, it can be used as an intermediate form in the process of recognition of wraparound variables.

```
j = m
do i = m, n
    a(j) = b(k)
    j = i + 1
    k = j
end do
```

⇒

```
k0 = k
CDOALL i = m,n
    a(i) = b((k0 - m) * 0 ** (i - m) + i)
END DO
```

Figure 4.13 Wraparound variables recognized by Parafrase-2.

The intermediate code generated by Parafrase-2 in Figure 4.13 is not meant to be the target code for execution, simply because it is inefficient and complex for dependence analysis. It is meant to illustrate the generality and precision of our semantic-based framework, and clearly indicates that no separate algorithm is required for recognition of wraparound variables.

The code fragment of Figure 4.14 shows the structure of the important loop nest of the program TRFD in Perfect Benchmarks®. The lower

INDUCTION VARIABLES

bound and the upper bound of the inner-most loop are generalized induction variables of the enclosing loops, as discovered by the symbolic analyzer of Parafrase-2. The upper bound, lmax, is a wraparound variable whose value at the first iteration of the inner-most loop matches the closed form found for the remaining iterations. Components of the source code that determine this property are shown in the frame boxes. Automatic induction analysis of this particular code is beyond the scope of other state-of-the-art parallelizing compilers of which we are aware.

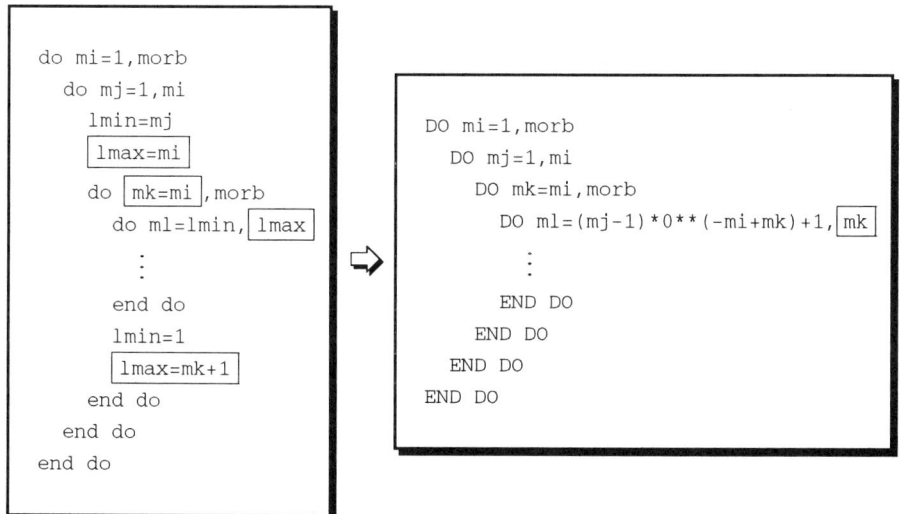

Figure 4.14 Wraparound variables in program TRFD.

Having symbolic values of expressions, the compiler first tries to find the function that interpolates the expression at all iterations of the loop. If the expression is not recognized as an induction expression, then the compiler tries to find a function that interpolates the expression at all but the first n iterations, for n varying from two to a limit set by the compiler or the user. If such a function is found, then that expression is a wraparound expression of the loop, characterized by the derived function. n iterations have to be peeled off the loop, and the number of iterations of the new loop is n less than that of the original one. In the case that the compiler cannot assure that the original loop would be executed for at least n iterations, the transformed code has to be augmented with conditional statements to avoid the execution of peeled iterations if they would not be executed in the original loop. Within our symbolic analysis framework, it is even possible to recognize cases where several distinct progression forms are interleaved with a period of ω iterations. In such cases, symbolic values that an expression assumes at iterations $i, i + \omega, i + 2\omega, \ldots$ can be described by a characteristic function.

4.6 LOOP NORMALIZATION

Since the description of data dependence tests is simpler when the stride of loops is one and the loop lower limit is a constant such as zero or one, many of the parallelizing compilers normalize loops. Loop normalization not only does not solve the dependence problem, but also complicates subscript expressions and can raise difficulties for dependence analysis. However, there are cases where loop normalization becomes necessary. The advantage and disadvantages of loop normalization for dependence testing has been studied by Girkar and Polychronopoulos [GP88], and by Wolfe [Wol93].

Parafrase-2 tries to avoid loop normalizations that complicate subscript expressions. Even in the cases where normalization becomes necessary, it is done in such a way that usually simplifies subscript expressions and thereafter dependence analysis. The greatest common divisor of the differences of characteristic functions of induction expressions at two consecutive iterations of the loop is used as the stride of the loop index variable.

For example, consider the source code shown in Figure 4.15. Parafrase-2 has chosen 2 as the stride of the loop, since 2 is the greatest common divisor of the strides of all of the loop induction expressions. Normalization of the loop complicates all subscript expressions, and a more precise dependence analysis will be required for loop parallelization. Parafrase-2 also tries not to generate temporary assignment statements, in the process of computing loop bounds, in order to avoid further need for privatization of these computations in the case of nested loops. Generation of temporary assignment statements for computing loop bounds, however, becomes necessary when loop bounds are complicated; in particular when loop bounds involve function calls with side effects whose complexity is beyond the compiler's analysis capability.

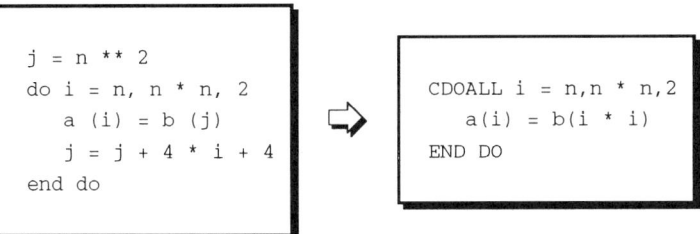

Figure 4.15 Selective normalization of loop bounds.

4.7 RECOGNITION OF LOOP-INVARIANT COMPUTATIONS

Loop-invariant expressions are of particular interest in optimizing compilers. Their recognition is a basis for *code motion* [CS70, Rei80], an important loop optimization technique that improves program performance by reducing frequency of execution of some instructions. In parallelizing compilers, on the other hand, recognition of loop-invariant expressions has an important role in dependence analysis. The fact that a symbolic term in an array subscript is loop-invariant might have a vital role in parallelization of the loop and can result in a significant performance gain. In many cases in which dependence equations contain unknown symbolic terms, a simple symbolic manipulation is sufficient for the purpose of dependence analysis, provided that the unknown symbolic terms are invariant in the loops under consideration [All83, HP91].

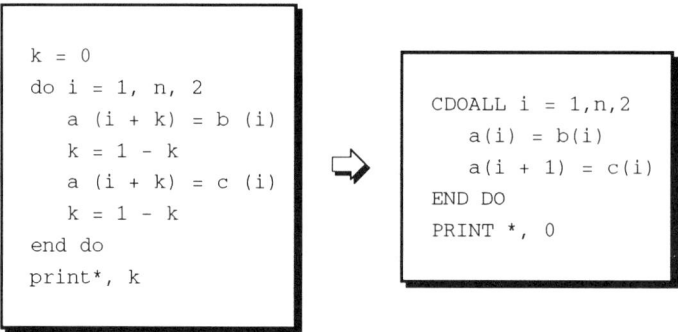

Figure 4.16 Loop-invariant expressions recognized by Parafrase-2.

Loop-invariant expressions and code motion can be considered as special cases of induction expressions and strength reduction. Loop-invariant expressions are induction expressions whose characteristic functions are independent of loop index variables. In fact, in our symbolic analysis framework, whose architecture is shown in Figure 4.17, recognition of loop-invariant expressions is a byproduct of induction expression analysis. This approach to loop-invariant expressions is more precise than traditional methods using *reaching definitions* based on *def-use chains* [ASU86]. To illustrate this, consider the code shown in Figure 4.16. Although variable *k* is modified within the loop, Parafrase-2 has discovered that all occurrences of *k* inside the loop are invariant. Syntactical methods are not able to recognize this class of loop-invariant expressions.

4.8 ARCHITECTURE OF A SYMBOLIC ANALYSIS SYSTEM

This section describes briefly the organization of the symbolic analysis system of Parafrase-2 and the interaction of its modules. A fundamental component of the system is a *symbolic interpreter* that interprets programs in a symbolic domain to discover their properties. The important

INDUCTION VARIABLES

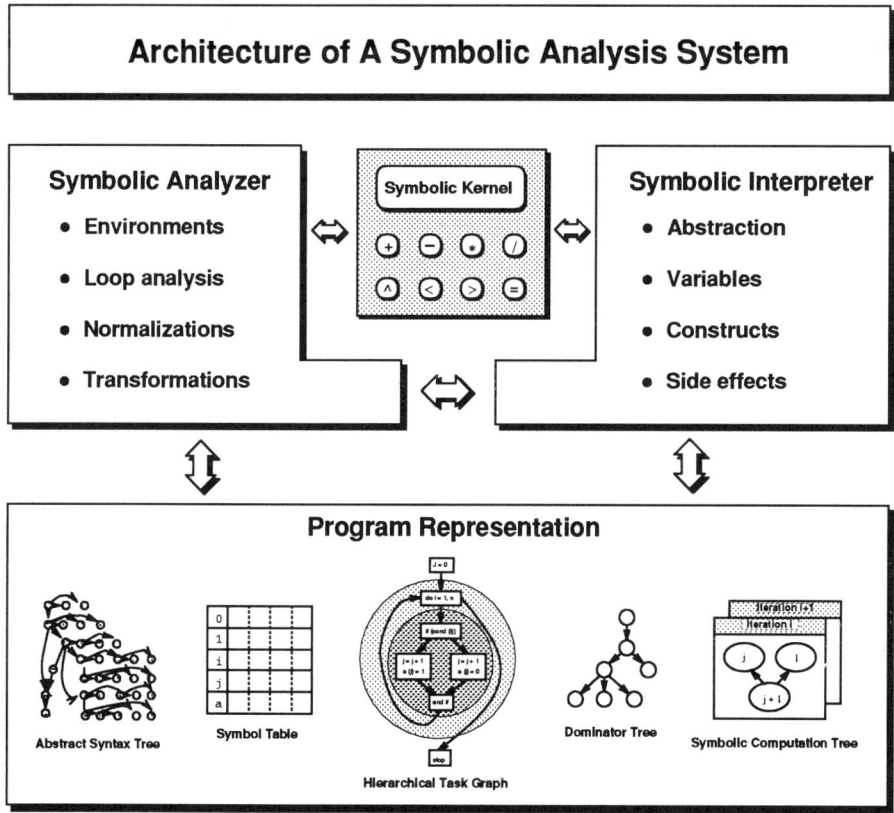

Figure 4.17 Symbolic analysis system of Parafrase-2.

function of the interpreter is the act of *abstraction*, i.e. the assignment of meaning to program constructs.

Programs are represented at various levels of abstraction. From a program's abstract syntax tree, the compiler derives a hierarchical representation of the program, by control flow analysis and by applying the normalizations discussed in Section 3.6.1. Within this hierarchy, program loops are identified, and loop nesting is well-defined.

A *symbolic analyzer* computes the context in which program constructs are interpreted. It also determines the invariant part of a context as the result of symbolic interpretation. This analysis is required for an efficient context propagation. Loop analysis is another important function of the symbolic analyzer. The symbolic interpreter executes the loop body using the invariant part of the context, and the symbolic analyzer identifies and solves the recurrences defined by the loop body. Then, the exit equation of the loop is solved by the symbolic analyzer, and the effect of loop execution is derived.

The abstract machine, on which the symbolic interpreter runs the program, is a *symbolic kernel*, a concise set of algebraic symbolic operations. The symbolic kernel employs mathematical tools such as number theory and mathematical induction in performing the symbolic operations.

This system provides a powerful framework for program analysis, parallelization, and optimization. One key feature of the analysis in this framework is its precision insensitivity to the order in which a variety of problems are solved. Its extensive analysis power, together with the efficiency of the employed techniques, distinguishes our symbolic analysis framework from the traditional data flow analysis frameworks.

5
INTERPROCEDURAL SYMBOLIC ANALYSIS

The presence of procedure calls complicates analysis of programs, and existing parallelizing compilers give up on dependence analysis of loops that contain procedure calls. In our program analysis framework, procedures are treated as abstract operators, and are modeled by their effects on program variables. Procedures are abstracted by closed form expressions that are solutions to the system of recurrences defined by their bodies. External side effects such as input/output statements are also taken into account. The derived knowledge about actual parameters of procedures can be used to simplify [Weg76a]or partially evaluate [JGS93] the procedures. Procedure specialization [CL73], also known as *procedure cloning* [CHK92], can be very beneficial in the enhancement and exploitation of the parallelism available in programs. There are, however, many efficiency issues and tradeoffs involved in interprocedural analysis. We do not discuss those issues here, instead, we give an example of interprocedural symbolic analysis in our framework, and refer the interested reader to the literature [CHK92, HMCCR93, Hav94, HK91, Iri93, TIF86].

Parallelization of a toy Fortran code using interprocedural symbolic analysis of Parafrase-2 is demonstrated in Figure 5.1. The loop of procedure test contains calls to procedures f and ndx. The dependences introduced by these procedures prevent parallelization of the loop in the caller procedure test. However, the symbolic analyzer of Parafrase-2

```
subroutine test (a,b,n)
real a (*), b (2 * n,*)
implicit integer (a-z)
m = 1
j = 1
k = 2
last = k
do i = 1, 2 * n
   call f (a(m),b(m,j))
   last = ndx (j, k, m)
end do
print*, last
end

subroutine f (x, y)
x = x + sqrt (abs (y))
y = x / (1 + y ** 2)
end

function ndx (j, k, m)
implicit integer (a-z)
tmp = j
j = k
k = tmp
m = m + 1
ndx = tmp
end
```

⇨

```
SUBROUTINE test(a,b,n)
INTEGER n
REAL a(*)
REAL b(2 * n,*)
INTEGER i

CDOALL i = 1,2 * n
   CALL f(a(i),b(i,((-1)**i+3)/2))
END DO
PRINT *, 2
END


SUBROUTINE f(x,y)
REAL x, y

x = x + sqrt(abs(y))
y = x / (1 + y ** 2)
END
```

Figure 5.1 Interprocedural symbolic analysis of Parafrase-2.

has been able to derive the exact function of the abstract operator ndx, and has used this information in the call to the procedure f. Exploitation of symbolic information about the parameters of procedure f has enabled the interprocedural dependence analyzer [Sch90] of Parafrase-2 to prove lack of dependence between calls to procedure f. Furthermore, after derivation of the exact side effects of procedure ndx the call to this procedure becomes useless and is eliminated by the compiler. Since there does not remain any dependence between loop iterations, the loop can run in parallel. This approach is especially useful in interprocedural dependence analysis techniques that summarize array accesses in terms of *regular sections* [HK91].

5.1 DEAD-CODE ELIMINATION

Exploitation of information that reaches a conditional statement may show that the condition is always *false* on all incoming control flow paths. In such a case, the *unreachable code* is identified. Ignoring the effects of unreachable codes, and eliminating them if possible, can increase the precision of program analysis. This is particularly important in interprocedural analysis schemes such as in-line expansion and procedure cloning, where properties of actual parameters are used to improve the performance of called procedures. Wegman and Zadeck [WZ91] have presented an algorithm for constant propagation combined with dead-code elimination. Their algorithm recognizes the same class of constants as that identified by Wegbreit's general global flow analysis algorithm [Weg75b]. However, their algorithm is based on the sparse representation of the *static single assignment* form, and is more efficient than Wegbreit's algorithm.

As mentioned in Section 3.5, in our symbolic analysis method each node is interpreted in the context of its live predecessors. Consequently, elimination of effects of unreachable code is automatically accomplished in our scheme. Moreover, the class of unreachable statements, and hence

```
if (n .gt. 0) then
   j = (n * (n + 1)) / 2
   k = 0
   do i = 1, n
      k = k + i
      print*, k
   end do
   m = 0
   do i = 1, n
      k2p = k ** 2 + i + 1
      if (j**2+i.gt.k2p) then
         m = m + 1
      else
         m = m + 2
         a (m) = 1
      end if
   end do
end if
```

⇨

```
IF (n .GT. 0) THEN
   DO i = 1,n
      PRINT *, (i+i*i)/2
   END DO
   CDOALL i = 1,n
      IF (.false.) THEN
      ELSE
         a(2*i) = 1
      END IF
   END DO
END IF
```

Figure 5.2 Dead-code elimination performed by Parafrase-2.

INTERPROCEDURAL SYMBOLIC ANALYSIS 63

subsequent opportunities for optimization and parallelization discovered by our method, is considerably much larger than that handled by other schemes. For example, consider the code shown in Figure 5.2. The second loop cannot be parallelized unless the dependences are resolved. On the other hand, the semantic information provided by symbolic analysis shows that the condition of the if statement is always *false*, and hence the statement that increments m by one is unreachable. The abstract interpreter ignores the dead code and discovers that variable m is *always* incremented by two in each iteration of the loop. By deriving the closed form of variable m in terms of the loop index variable i, the compiler further eliminates the useless computation of k2p and the increment of m by two. As a result, no other dependences remain between various iterations of the loop, and the loop can run in parallel. Were the compiler unable to discover the fact that the increment of m by one is unreachable, full parallelization of the loop would be impossible. It is worth noting that in our symbolic analysis algorithm each node of the control flow graph is visited only once. Thus, propagation of information, induction analysis, and dead-code elimination are performed in a single application of the algorithm.

5.2 SYMBOLIC DEPENDENCE ANALYSIS

The effectiveness of parallelizing compilers and other parallel programming tools depend solely on the accuracy and effectiveness of their data dependence analysis techniques. Although powerful dependence analysis techniques have been employed in commercial and experimental systems, all these schemes fail in the presence of unknown symbolic terms that are not constant in the loops under consideration. In our study on Perfect Benchmarks®, summarized in Table 5.1, we found that close to 75% of loops in these programs had symbolic bounds. Also, a large percentage of array references in these benchmarks contain symbolic terms other than enclosing loop index variables. Parallelizing compilers handle some of these cases by applying classical optimization techniques such as constant propagation, induction variable substitution, and forward substitution. Nevertheless, standard dependence tests cannot be applied in many of the unresolved cases, owing to lack of information about the value of certain variables at compile time. Symbolic techniques are required for effective dependence analysis of these cases [All83, Iri93, Jou87, LT88, TIF86]. Our proposed symbolic analysis framework [HP91] supports a very accurate dependence analysis scheme in the presence of unknown symbolic terms.

The techniques presented in this book enable the compiler to express the important parameters of dependence analysis in terms of program invariants and loop index variables. These parameters include loop bound expressions and array index variables. By doing so, the difficult problem of dependence analysis reduces to a well-formulated mathematical problem, namely, existence of solution to the dependence equation, which is much simpler to solve than the original problem. It is much easier to reason about a *mathematical function* than to reason about a *computable function* described by a procedure in a programming language.

After collecting the required information by symbolic analysis, the compiler can perform *dependence testing* from a catalogue of dependence testing techniques [GKT91, MHL91] ranging from efficient heuristics [Ban88] to exact and potentially expensive integer programming techniques [Fea88, Pug91]. Thus, symbolic analysis serves as a basis for new dependence testing techniques as well as more effective implementation of the known methods. In the following example, we introduce an efficient monotonicity test that can be used in dependence analysis. Monotonic functions are of particular importance in dependence analysis of regular programs, and sharp bounds on their range can be obtained easily[1].

---

[1] See Appendix A.

Table 5.1 Symbolic terms in Perfect Benchmarks®.

Program Name	% of Loops with Symbolic Bounds	% of Subscripts with Symbolic Terms
ADM	98	35
ARC2D	95	60
BDNA	69	47
DYFESM	85	26
FLO52	89	37
MDG	67	26
MG3D	100	89
OCEAN	93	45
QCD	67	18
SPEC77	24	38
TRACK	44	16
TRFD	72	41
Total	74	43

A performance metric, or cost estimate, could be used as a guide in choosing the appropriate dependence testing scheme from a catalogue of available ones. The performance prediction technique that we shall study in Chapter 6 is an important component of the framework. The cost estimate of a program loop indicates the importance of the loop, and helps the compiler to choose the required precision of dependence testing, and thus, the dependence technique itself, on a case-by-case basis.

Example **5.2.1** The code segment shown in Figure 4.4 is an example that requires symbolic dependence analysis. After elimination of the generalized induction variable `mijkl`, the subscript of array `xijkl` in Figure 4.5 is a nonlinear function of the enclosing loop index variables, and contains an unknown symbolic term, `num`. Another unknown symbolic term, `morb`, also appears in the enclosing loop bounds.

However, the compiler can use the following lemma, which is based on finite differences, to find a set of constraints sufficient to prove that the value of the subscript expression of the array xijkl is strictly increasing. Verification of these conditions at compile time indicates lack of dependences. If the compiler is not able to prove the validity of these conditions, they may be verified at run time to support a multi-version code.

LEMMA **5.2.1** *Suppose that L is a nest of depth n of unit stride loops, indexed by $\mathbf{i} = (i_1, i_2, \cdots, i_n)$, and characterized by the loop bounds $L_j \leq i_j \leq U_j$ for $1 \leq j \leq n$, where L_j and U_j are integer-valued functions of $i_1, i_2, \cdots, i_{j-1}$. Given an expression $e = f(i_1, i_2, \cdots, i_n)$, let $\Delta^j e = f(\mathbf{t}(\mathbf{i},j)) - f(\mathbf{s}(\mathbf{i},j)), \forall j : 1 \leq j \leq n$, where $\mathbf{s} = (s_1, s_2, \cdots, s_n)$ and $\mathbf{t} = (t_1, t_2, \cdots, t_n)$ are n-tuple vectors defined as follows:*

$$s_k(\mathbf{i},j) = \begin{cases} i_k & k \leq j \\ U_k(s_1(\mathbf{i},j), s_2(\mathbf{i},j), \cdots, s_{k-1}(\mathbf{i},j)) & j < k \leq n \end{cases}$$

$$t_k(\mathbf{i},j) = \begin{cases} i_k & k < j \\ i_k + 1 & k = j \\ L_k(t_1(\mathbf{i},j), t_2(\mathbf{i},j), \cdots, t_{k-1}(\mathbf{i},j)) & j < k \leq n \end{cases}$$

The expression e is strictly $\begin{cases} \text{increasing} & \text{if } \Delta^j e > 0 \\ \text{decreasing} & \text{if } \Delta^j e < 0 \end{cases}$ $\forall j : 1 \leq j \leq n.$

PROOF. Let $\mathcal{S}$ be the lexicographically ordered iteration space of the loop nest and l its largest element, then we have

$$\mathcal{S} = \left\{ (i_1, i_2, \cdots, i_n) \mid \bigwedge_{j=1}^{n} L_j(i_1, i_2, \cdots, i_{j-1}) \leq i_j \leq U_j(i_1, i_2, \cdots, i_{j-1}) \right\}.$$

Let the function $N : \mathcal{S} - \{l\} \to \mathcal{S}$ assigns to each element of $\mathcal{S} - \{l\}$ its immediate successor in the iteration space, then we have

$$N(\mathbf{i}) = \mathbf{j} \Leftrightarrow (\mathbf{j} \succ \mathbf{i}) \wedge (\mathbf{k} \succ \mathbf{i}) \Rightarrow \mathbf{k} \succeq \mathbf{j}.$$

To prove the first part of the lemma, it suffices to show that $f(N(\mathbf{i})) > f(\mathbf{i}), \forall \mathbf{i} \in \mathcal{S} - \{1\}$. For any $\mathbf{i} \in \mathcal{S} - \{1\}$, by the *well-ordering principle*, there exists a smallest j such that $\mathbf{i} = \mathbf{s}(\mathbf{i}, j)$. For such a j, from the definitions of $\mathcal{S}, \mathbf{s}$, and $\mathbf{t}$, $N(\mathbf{i}) = \mathbf{t}(\mathbf{i}, j)$. So, we have to show that $f(\mathbf{t}(\mathbf{i}, j)) > f(\mathbf{s}(\mathbf{i}, j))$. But this is immediate from the hypothesis, since $f(\mathbf{t}(\mathbf{i}, j)) - f(\mathbf{s}(\mathbf{i}, j)) > 0, \forall j : 1 \leq j \leq n$.

The proof of the *strictly decreasing* part of the lemma is very similar to the above, and is omitted. □

In the code segment of Figure 4.5, let the value of the subscript expression of the array xijkl at the iteration (mi, mj, mk, ml) be denoted by $e(mi, mj, mk, ml)$. By applying Lemma 5.2.1, we get:

1. $\Delta^1 e = (mi^2 + 3mi - morb^2 - morb + num^2 + num + 4)/2$,
2. $\Delta^2 e = (mi^2 + mi - morb^2 - morb + num^2 + num + 2)/2$,
3. $\Delta^3 e = 1$,
4. $\Delta^4 e = 1$.

$\Delta^3 e$ and $\Delta^4 e$ are trivially greater than zero. In the program TRFD, when the subprogram that contains the above code segment is called, the variable morb has the same value as num. Thus, the constraints for parallelization of the loops reduce to $mi^2 + 3mi + 4 > 0$ and $mi^2 + mi + 2 > 0$. These conditions are also satisfied inside the loop since $mi > 0$. In fact, these conditions are satisfied for all $mi \in \mathbb{Z}$. Hence, the compiler concludes that the sequence of values that the expression e assumes in successive iterations of the loops of Figure 4.5 is strictly increasing, and all the loops can run in parallel.

5.3 PROGRAM OPTIMIZATION

Symbolic analysis can be used as a basis for a wide range of program optimizations such as strength reduction, restructuring of arithmetic computations, and elimination of redundant computations.

5.3.1 Generalized Strength Reduction

Strength reduction is a compiler technique that replaces expensive operations by fast instructions [ACK81]. The classical strength reduction algorithm is based on induction variable detection. A pattern matching approach is used to remove multiplications of induction variables by region constants or other induction variables. Any arbitrary polynomial of induction variables can be reduced by multiple applications of the algorithm. However, multiple invocations of the algorithm will create a large amount of intermediate code for polynomials with many terms.

Strength reduction technique can be generalized by considering computations in their entirety rather than their partial computations that appear in their functional definitions [HP92]. Using the information gathered by symbolic analysis, the compiler can basically perform the inverse of induction variable substitution. This technique has the power of transforming the code segments of Figure 4.4 and Figure 4.5 to the one shown in the Figure 5.3 in the case that the compiler decides to run all the enclosing loops sequentially.

This scheme when applied selectively to a nest of sequential and parallel loops, reduces the operations in the sequential loops, while it does not prohibit the concurrent execution of parallel loops. In other words, computations involving induction variables are distributed over loops in such a way as to get the computations done with the minimal amount of work. We applied this technique to the manually parallelized [EHJ[+]91] version of the loop nest of program TRFD shown

INTERPROCEDURAL SYMBOLIC ANALYSIS 69

```
mi2 = 0
mleft = (num * (num + 1) - morb * (morb + 1)) / 2
mijkl = 0
DO mi = 1,morb
   mijkl = mijkl + mi
   mi2 = mi2 + mi
   DO mj = 1,mi
      DO mk = mi + 1,morb
         DO ml = 1,mk
            mijkl = mijkl + 1
            xijkl (mijkl) = xkl (ml)
         END DO
      END DO
      mijkl = mijkl + mi2 + mleft
   END DO
END DO
END
```

Figure 5.3 Generalized strength reduction of Figure 4.5.

in Figure 4.4, and got a speedup of 20% on Cedar. This speedup is the result of optimizing the computations related to just one induction variable, i.e. `mijkl`.

5.3.2 Restructuring of Arithmetic Computations

To evaluate an arithmetic expression under a set of algebraic laws, the compiler can generate code for any equivalent expression, obtained by successive applications of the algebraic laws [GJ82]. An optimality criterion can be defined based on the cost of computations. In the general case, finding an optimal solution of code generation has been proven to be NP-Complete. However, for the cases where the DAG representation of expressions is a tree, efficient algorithms exist that find an optimal solution for machines that have a single instruction stream [ASU86]. In many cases where the DAG representation of expressions is not a tree, symbolic values of expressions may be used to find an equivalent tree of the DAG and thus generate the optimal code.

6
TIMING ANALYSIS AND SCHEDULING

Optimizing compilers in general, and parallelizing compilers in particular, try to improve the performance of programs by performing a series of transformations. A transformation is an optimization if a set (possibly empty) of conditions is satisfied. These conditions are derived from a comparison of the cost functions of the original and the transformed code. The ideal cost function is the real execution time of the program, which in the case of an arbitrary program is not computable even if its data are given. Therefore, it is essential to find heuristics for estimating the execution time of programs at various granularity levels, for example program, subprogram, loop, basic block, statement, and expression.

Symbolic analysis supports the capability of program performance prediction. It can derive closed form expressions for the running time of many programs in terms of their input data. In the case of conditional branches, symbolic analysis may be able to find the branch probabilities, provided that the conditions are based on the structural properties of the data, such as *shape* and *size*. Symbolic analysis can even provide statistical information such as *minimum, maximum, average*, and *standard deviation* of the execution time of iterations of program loops. Such a metric for analysis of algorithms is proposed by Knuth [Knu73], and used by Wegbreit [Weg75a, Weg76b], the Cousots [CC77], Ramshaw [Ram79], and Hickey and Cohen [HC88].

Semi-automatic worst-case analysis of a large class of logic program is studied by Debray and Lin [DL93].

The performance measure should also take into account architectural issues such as the type of memory accesses in computers with hierarchical memories. In parallelizing compilers, the performance measure is especially useful for choosing the appropriate set of transformations and scheduling strategies. In the case of dynamic scheduling, the compiler can use the generalized strength reduction scheme of Section 5.3 to instrument the code in such a way, so that each task of the program's *Hierarchical Task Graph (HTG)* [Gir91, GP92] has its own metric computed in an efficient way. In the following sections we describe how timing information can guide scheduling and how such information can be computed by compilers using symbolic techniques.

6.1 LOOP SCHEDULING

One of the most thoroughly investigated problems in parallel processing has been that of extracting and utilizing loop-level parallelism. The fact that it remains one of the most active problems is a testament to its importance, as well as to the adequacy (or lack thereof) of existing solutions. The main issue in the scheduling of parallel loops is the tradeoff between balancing the processors' load and minimizing scheduling overhead. At one extreme, a strategy called *self-scheduling* [TY86] schedules loop iterations one at a time, and thus achieves the best possible load balancing. However, self-scheduling is not a good scheme if the overhead involved with each dispatch is comparable to the average execution time of the iterations. At the other extreme, another scheme, *chunk scheduling* [KW85], allocates a fixed number of iterations (a chunk) to each idle processor. This method reduces the scheduling overhead but may result in poor performance when there is a considerable variation between execution times of loop iterations. This may be due to the structure of computations in each iteration, or it could be the result of unpredictable

TIMING ANALYSIS AND SCHEDULING

characteristics of the computing system such as network latency or cache performance. Between these two schemes lie other approaches that attempt to compromise between load balancing and minimizing overhead. *Guided self-scheduling* [PK87], *factoring* [FFH90, FHSF92], and *trapezoidal self-scheduling* [TN91] are examples of such schemes.

```
n = 50
DOALL i = 1, n*n
    INTEGER k
    DO k = i, n*n
        a(i) = a(i)+x*b(k)*c(k-1)
    END DO
END DOALL
```

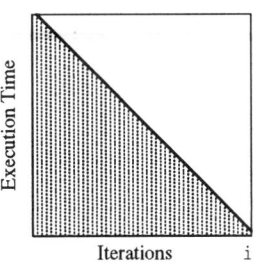

Figure 6.1 Adjoint-convolution program and its parallel work.

All the above schemes can benefit from the cost estimates provided by the symbolic analysis. We demonstrate this by modifying the chunk scheduling scheme to utilize the symbolic execution time information. We call this new scheme *balanced chunk scheduling* (or BCS) [HP93, HP94]. The performance of balanced chunk scheduling will be compared with that of chunk scheduling and self-scheduling. The reported performance is the result of compiling and running our examples on a system developed at the University of Illinois [Mor95].

It is oftentimes the characteristics of loop iterations that make one scheduling scheme perform better than another. In the case of coarse-grained iterations with variable execution times, self-scheduling performs much better than chunk scheduling, while fine-grained iterations with constant execution time favor chunk scheduling. To compare the performance of balanced chunk scheduling against other schemes, we have selected two examples from [FHSF92] that cover a wide spectrum of characteristics. The benchmark program shown in Figure 6.1 is an *adjoint-convolution*. The granularity of the parallel work is large, with a great deal of variance among the parallel iterations. On the other hand, the parallel loop of the Gauss-Jordan linear equation solver shown in Figure 6.2, has a small granularity of parallel work with a very small variance in iteration length.

```
DO i = 1, n
   DOALL ip = 1, n*(n-i+1)
      INTEGER j, k
      j = (ip-1)/(n-i+1)+1
      k = i+ip-(n-i+1)*((ip-1)/(n-i+1))
      IF (i .NE. j) THEN
         a(j,k)=a(j,k)-(a(j,i)*a(i,k))*a(i,i)
      END IF
   END DOALL
END DO
```

Figure 6.2 Gauss-Jordan program and its parallel work.

6.1.1 Balanced Chunk Scheduling

In this section, we outline a novel and radically different approach to the problem of loop scheduling which is based on symbolic program analysis. The net result is the ability to statically partition irregular loops with variable size body into a set of unequal partitions; thus achieving load balancing that only the most flexible dynamic heuristics can achieve, but without incurring the run-time overhead. The same principles are used to partition a loop into equal workload (as opposed to equal size) activities at run-time. The fundamental properties of this approach establish it as the most robust and generally efficient solution to loop-level scheduling for gang-scheduling environments.

To schedule a loop with N iterations on P processors, chunk scheduling would allocate roughly N/P iterations to each processor. This may result in an unbalanced load if there is a large variance between execution times of the iterations. However, if the compiler has the cost estimate of

TIMING ANALYSIS AND SCHEDULING

an arbitrary iteration i, as a function of i, then the loop can be partioned into P chunks such that the amount of work in each chunk is equal or approximately equal. This results in a balanced load while keeping the overhead minimal. Note that assigning blocks of successive iterations to processors has other advantages such as increasing the chance of spatial locality and strength reduction. An example of such a partition is shown in Figure 6.3 for a given workload and four processors.

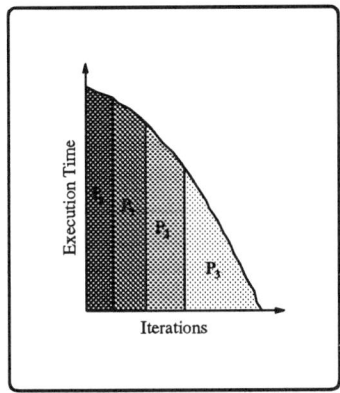

Figure 6.3 A loop partition to chunks of equal workload.

When the number of processors and total number of iterations of a loop are known at compile time, an auto-scheduling compiler might be able to do the above scheduling statically and thus avoid the run-time overhead. The adjoint-convolution program, discussed earlier, is such a case. The corresponding transformation for balanced chunk scheduling on four processors is shown in Figure 6.4. In the transformed code, there are as many iterations of the parallel loop as the number of processors, four iterations in this case. Furthermore, the workload of each processor is almost equal to that of the others.

In more complicated cases, an auto-scheduling compiler can insert the appropriate code to do the loop partitioning at run time. For example, consider the Gauss-Jordan program shown in Figure 6.2. The total number of iterations of the parallel loop is not a constant; rather it

```
n = 50
DOALL i = 1, n*n
    INTEGER k
    DO k = i, n*n
        a(i)=a(i)+x*b(k)*c(k-1)
    END DO
END DOALL
```

⇨

```
INTEGER iter (5), p
DATA iter /1,336,733,1251,2501/
DOALL p = 1, 4
    INTEGER i, k
    DO i = iter(p), iter(p+1)-1
        DO k = i, 2500
            a(i)=a(i)+x*b(k)*c(k-1)
        END DO
    END DO
END DOALL
```

Figure 6.4 A transformation that balances workload.

is equal to n*(n-i+1), where n is the problem size and i is the enclosing loop index variable. Hence, it is not possible to partition this parallel loop with the static scheme used in the previous example. However, the compiler can transform the Gauss-Jordan program to the one shown in Figure 6.5. The shaded code segment partitions the parallel loop into chunks of equal workload. Note that strength reduction discussed earlier has a direct application here. It has been used to efficiently partition the parallel loop.

For both the Gauss-Jordan and adjoint-convolution programs, the performance of balanced chunk scheduling is compared with self-scheduling and chunk scheduling in Figure 6.6. For the reasons discussed earlier, in the case of the Gauss-Jordan program self-scheduling results in a poor performance. Similarly, chunk scheduling results in a poor speedup in the case of the adjoint-convolution program. However, in both cases balanced chunk scheduling results in consistently high performance. This also indicates that symbolic cost estimates can be used to design robust scheduling strategies that perform very well on a wide range of cases. Sarkar has studied partitioning of parallel programs using cost estimates computed from profile information [Sar89a, Sar89b].

TIMING ANALYSIS AND SCHEDULING 77

```
INTEGER iter (p+1)
INTEGER p, start, this
np1 = n + 1
pp1 = p + 1
iter (1) = 1
work = n * n
DO i = 1, n

        load = work
        iter (pp1) = work + 1
        work = work - n
        start = 1
        procs = p
        DO ix = 2, p
            this = load / procs + 0.5
            procs = procs - 1
            load = load - this
            start = start + this
            iter (ix) = start
        END DO

    DOALL ix = 1, p
        INTEGER ip, j, k
        DO ip = iter (ix), iter (ix+1) - 1
            j = (ip - 1) / (np1 - i) + 1
            k = i + ip - (np1 - i) * ((ip - 1) / (np1 - i))
            IF (i .NE. j) THEN
                a (j,k)=a(j,k)-(a(j,i)*a(i,k))/a(i,i)
            END IF
        END DO
    END DOALL
END DO
```

Figure 6.5 Dynamic load balancing of a parallel loop.

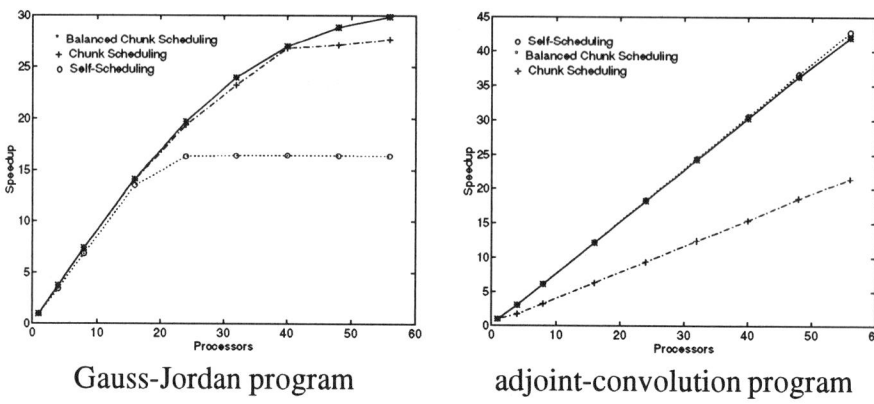

Gauss-Jordan program   adjoint-convolution program

Figure 6.6 Performance of various scheduling schemes.

6.2 DERIVATION OF SYMBOLIC COST ESTIMATES

Deriving cost estimates of program tasks at any level in terms of their inputs is essentially the same as finding the net effect of execution of the tasks on a variable which is initially zero, and is incremented by the cost of each operation. This problem is clearly unsolvable in the general case, otherwise the *halting problem* [GJ79] would have been decidable. However, many instances of this problem are solvable. For example, consider the code shown in Figure 6.7. This subroutine, taken from *Numerical Recipes* [PTTF92], is a complete Cholesky decomposition for solving linear equations.

We illustrate how timing analysis of this program may be performed in our symbolic analysis framework by showing the derivation of the total number of assignment statements executed in this subroutine. Suppose that there were assignment statements in the program to initialize a variable `nmasgn` to zero, and to increment it by one for each assignment statement in the program. These statements, shown in frames, do not have to be instrumented in the source code; we have done so just for presenting the concept. The total number of assignment statements executed by this program is equal to the final value of the variable `nmasgn`. Parafrase-2 has been able to derive this value, as shown in the `print` statement. The induction analysis performed in this case requires the compiler's capability of recognizing conditional non-linear induction variables with multiple assignments.

```
subroutine choldc (a, n, np, p)
integer n, np
real a (np, np), p (n)
integer i, j, k
real sum

nmasgn=0
do i = 1, n
  do j = i, n
    sum=a(i,j)
    nmasgn=nmasgn+1
    do k = i-1, 1, -1
      sum=sum-a(i,k)*a(j,k)
      nmasgn=nmasgn+1
    end do
    if(i.eq.j) then
      if(sum.le.0) pause 'failed.'
      p(i)=sqrt(sum)
      nmasgn=nmasgn+1
    else
      a(j,i)=sum/p(i)
      nmasgn=nmasgn+1
    end if
  end do
end do
print*, nmasgn
end
```

⇨

```
SUBROUTINE choldc(a,n,np,p)
INTEGER n, np
REAL a(np,np)
REAL p(n)
INTEGER i, j, k
REAL sum

DO i = 1,n
  DO j = i,n
    sum=a(i,j)
    DO k = i - 1,1, -1
      sum=sum-a(i,k)*a(j,k)
    END DO
    IF(i.EQ.j) THEN
      IF(sum.LE.0) PAUSE 'failed.
      p(i)=sqrt(sum)
    ELSE
      a(j,i)=sum/p(i)
    END IF
  END DO
END DO
PRINT *, (5*n+6*n*n+n**3)/6
END
```

Figure 6.7 Timing analysis of a Cholesky decomposition.

Had we wanted more detailed information, for example the total number of multiplications or array references, it would have been as simple. The important point in this approach is that the execution cost of each iteration of a loop can be derived as a function of the loop index variable.

Conditional statements can be major obstacles in timing analysis. We divide conditional statements into two categories; statements with *structural*conditions, and statements with *data dependent*conditions. Conditional statements whose conditions are functions of only enclosing loop index variables and loop invariants belong to the former category. Below, we present a method for timing analysis of a large class of structural conditions. With this approach and current capabilities of Parafrase-2, we were able to do the symbolic timing analysis of the program TRFD from Perfect Benchmarks®. For all components of TRFD, Parafrase-2 was able to automatically derive the timing complexities. It estimated the total number of floating point operations of TRFD to be 430.878M. The actual number of floating point operations of TRFD, obtained with the hardware performance monitor on a Cray X-MP, is 430.877M. The slight difference is the result of approximations in the cases of data dependent conditional branches. Timing analysis of programs with data dependent conditions requires statistical knowledge of distribution of the input data [Koz81], and is beyond the scope of this book.

Suppose that the compiler wants to compute the total number of floating point multiplications in the example shown in Figure 6.8, a code that contains a structural conditional statement. The total number of floating point multiplications performed by the unconditional assignment statement is equal to $\sum_{i=1}^{n} \sum_{j=1}^{i} \sum_{k=1}^{i} 1$, which is equal to $n(n+1)(2n+1)/6$. This computation may be carried on by the compiler capability of handling generalized induction variables. More precisely, the compiler can compute this function by assuming a variable, which has been initialized to zero, is incremented by one at the point where the unconditional multiplication is performed. The closed formula for the value of that variable, after execution of the entire loop nest, gives the total number of unconditional floating point multiplications.

Computing the total number of floating point multiplications performed by the conditional assignment statement requires more analysis. This corresponds to a *conditional induction variable* which can be computed

TIMING ANALYSIS AND SCHEDULING

precisely in this example. The convex polytope associated with the whole iteration space of the loops is also shown in Figure 6.8. The total number of points inside the convex polytope which have integer coordinates is equal to the total number of times that the unconditional floating point multiplication is performed, and is computed above. On the other hand, the convex polytope corresponding to the *then* part of the *if* statement is shaded, and its total number of points with integer coordinates equals the total number of times that the conditional floating point multiplication has been performed. This number is equal to $\sum_{i=1}^{n} \left(\sum_{j=1}^{i} \sum_{k=1}^{j} 1 \right) + i - 1$, which is equal to $n(n^2 + 6n - 1)/6$. Hence, the total number of floating point multiplications in the code segment of Figure 6.8 equals to $n(n+1)(2n+1)/6 + n(n^2 + 6n - 1)/6$, or $(n^3 + 3n^2)/2$.

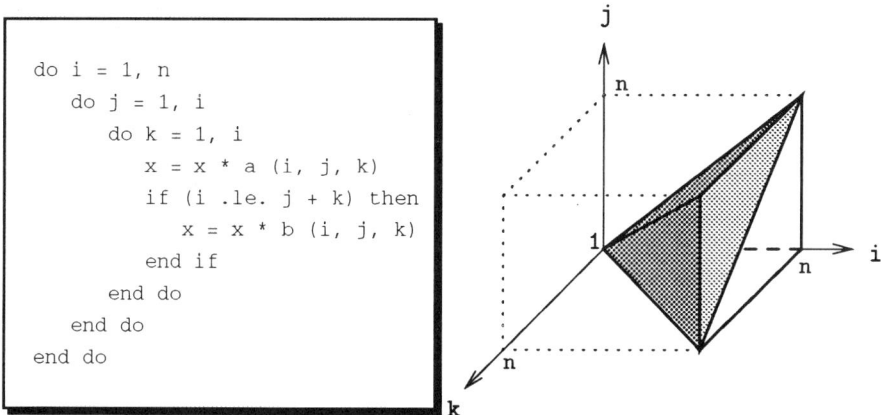

Figure 6.8 A code segment and its associated convex polytopes.

In cases where the exact number of points in a convex polytope cannot be found, or an estimate would suffice, the probability of conditional branches can be computed as the ratio of the volume of the corresponding convex polytope of the branch, to that of the conditional statement itself. Computing the volume of convex sets, in the general case, is proven to be an exponential problem in terms of the dimension of the convex set [BF86]. Even the probabilistic algorithm for finding the Euclidian volume of convex bodies, proposed in [DFK91], which has a polynomial time complexity is computationally very expensive. However, the convex polytopes that we consider have a nice property that makes computation of their volumes much easier. In the mathematical sense, these polytopes are special cases of *cylinders*. An algebraic approach to the problem is discussed in the next section.

6.3 COMPUTING PROBABILITIES OF STRUCTURAL CONDITIONS

In this section we discuss the problem of the enumeration of points of a convex polytope in which a condition is satisfied. The frame of the convex polytope is defined by the bounds of a given loop nest, and the condition is a boolean function of the loop index variables. The problem of *zero-trip loops* is one of the simplest instances of the above general problem.

6.3.1 Zero-trip Loops

Consider the program segment shown in Figure 6.9. Given arbitrary arithmetic functions f and g, it is impossible for a compiler to compute the final value of k in a closed form as a function of n, even if h is a constant such as 1, and f and g are restricted to be polynomials. The reason is that we need to know the ranges of i, for which $g(i) \geq f(i)$. That means, we have to be able to solve $g(i) - f(i) \geq 0$. But, it is a well known fact in algebra [Hun74] that for any $n \geq 5$, there are polynomials of degree n with integer coefficients whose roots cannot be expressed in terms of radicals of roots of polynomials of degrees ≤ 4.

The above problem, however, can be solved in many cases that occur in real applications. An equivalent problem in combinatorics is evaluation

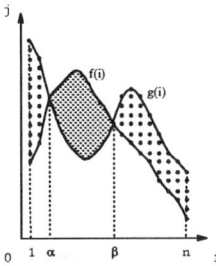

Figure 6.9 A nested loop and its iteration space.

of nested sums with the possibility that the lower bounds might be greater than their upper bounds. A very simple example of this case is $\sum_{i=1}^{n} 1$. This sum is equal to n only if n is not negative; otherwise the sum is zero by definition. More generally, if $g(k) = \sum_{i=0}^{k} f_i$, $\forall k \geq 0$, then $\sum_{i=m}^{n} f_i = g(n) - g(m-1)$, $\forall n \geq m$. However, if $n < m$, then $\sum_{i=m}^{n} f_i = 0$, and $g(n) - g(m-1)$ will not necessarily be zero. In fact $g(n) - g(m-1) = -\sum_{i=n+1}^{m-1} f_i$ in case $n < m$.

Existing symbolic algebra packages do not handle such cases properly. Basically, their methods for computing sums are based on some implicit assumptions which are not verified, and might even be invalid. For example, *Maple* evaluates $\sum_{i=1}^{n} \sum_{j=10}^{i} 1$ to be $n(n-17)/2$. For $n = 10$, $\sum_{i=1}^{n} \sum_{j=10}^{i} 1$ is mathematically defined to be equal to 1, while $10(10-17)/2 = -35$. Unfortunately, this is the way that the function $\sum$ is defined in *Maple*. On the other hand, the current *SymbolicSum* package of *Mathematica* does not derive a closed form for this summation unless either applications of *SymbolicSum* are nested, or the value of n is given. In the former case, *Mathematica* derives the same incorrect closed formula as *Maple*, and in the latter case, the time spent to compute the summation is directly proportional to the value of n, as computation is carried on by direct enumeration.

To solve the above problems efficiently, the algebra of conditional values is introduced in the following section.

6.4 ALGEBRA OF CONDITIONAL VALUES

DEFINITION **6.4.1** The *truth*function $\tau : \{\text{FALSE}, \text{TRUE}\} \to \{0,1\} \subset \mathbb{R}$ is defined as [1]:

$$\tau(b) = \begin{cases} 1 & \text{if } b = \text{TRUE}, \\ 0 & \text{otherwise}. \end{cases}$$

COROLLARY **6.4.1** For any $a, b \in \{\text{FALSE}, \text{TRUE}\}$, the following hold:

1. $\tau(a) + \tau(\bar{a}) = 1$.
2. $\tau(a)\,\tau(\bar{a}) = 0$.
3. $\tau(a \wedge b) = \tau(a)\,\tau(b)$.
4. $\tau(a \vee b) = \tau(a) + \tau(b) - \tau(a \wedge b)$.

PROOF. If a is TRUE, then $\bar{a}$ is FALSE, $\tau(a)$ is one, $\tau(\bar{a})$ is zero, and both relations 1 and 2 hold. Similarly, if a is FALSE, then $\bar{a}$ is TRUE, $\tau(a)$ is zero, $\tau(\bar{a})$ is one, and again both relations 1 and 2 hold.

If either a or b is FALSE, then $a \wedge b$ is also FALSE, and both sides of relation 3 are equal to zero. On the other hand, if both a and b are TRUE, then $a \wedge b$ is also TRUE, and both sides of relation 3 are equal to one. Therefore relation 3 holds for all possible values of a and b.

Relation 4 can be proven using the relations $1, 3$ and *DeMorgan's law* as follows:

$$\begin{aligned}
\tau(a \vee b) &= \tau(\overline{\bar{a} \wedge \bar{b}}) \stackrel{1}{=} 1 - \tau(\bar{a} \wedge \bar{b}) \stackrel{3}{=} 1 - \tau(\bar{a})\,\tau(\bar{b}) \\
&\stackrel{1}{=} 1 - (1 - \tau(a))(1 - \tau(b)) \stackrel{3}{=} \tau(a) + \tau(b) - \tau(a \wedge b).
\end{aligned}$$

□

---
[1] Following Iverson's APL convention, Knuth [Knu92] suggests the notation $[b]$ for $\tau(b)$.

TIMING ANALYSIS AND SCHEDULING

The function τ is simple, but very powerful. Many mathematical functions, including *abs, max, min, sign, positive part, negative part,* and *Kronecker delta,* can be easily defined by τ. A special case of the function τ is particularly useful for mechanical manipulation of relations between program variables. Given the set of program variables, a compiler may need to verify an element of B, the set of boolean expressions defined on the program variables using the two binary operations $\wedge$ and $\vee$, and the unary operation complement '¬', with the two binary constants TRUE and FALSE. Elements of B are formed by relational operations, or their complements, on the arithmetic expressions. Examples of such elements are: $x = 0$, $2x + 3y \leq z$, $(x \leq y) \vee (y \neq z)$, etc. As we shall see later, these constraints may be guards of such values as results of finite summations. For systematic manipulation of summations, a special case of the function τ is defined as follows:

DEFINITION **6.4.2** The *unit step* function $\mu : \mathbb{R} \to \{0,1\}$ is defined as:

$$\mu(x) = \tau(x > 0).$$

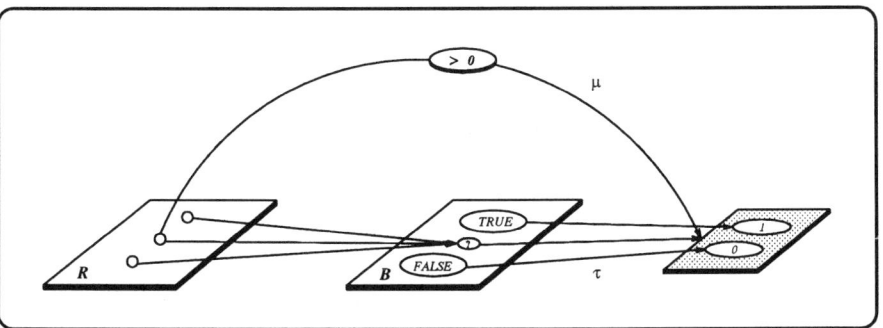

Figure 6.10 The *truth* and *unit step* functions.

Figure 6.10 shows a diagrammatic representation of the functions τ and μ, and distinguishes their domains. The following properties of μ, and the relations between μ and τ, are helpful in finding values of the *truth* functions of boolean expressions involving relational operations.

COROLLARY **6.4.2** For any $x \in \mathbb{R}$, the following hold:

1. $\mu(\alpha x) = \begin{cases} \mu(x) & \text{if } \alpha > 0, \\ 0 & \text{if } \alpha = 0, \\ \mu(-x) & \text{otherwise.} \end{cases}$

2. $\mu(xy) = \mu(x)\mu(y) + \mu(-x)\mu(-y)$.

3. $[\mu(x)]^n = \mu(x), \forall n \in \mathbb{P}$.

4. $\mu(x)\mu(-x) = 0$.

5. $\mu(x)x = max(x, 0)$.

6. $\tau(x > 0) = \mu(x)$.

7. $\tau(x < 0) = \mu(-x)$.

8. $\tau(x = 0) = 1 - \mu(x) - \mu(-x)$.

9. $\tau(x \geq 0) = 1 - \mu(-x)$.

10. $\tau(x \leq 0) = 1 - \mu(x)$.

11. $\tau(x \neq 0) = \mu(x) + \mu(-x)$.

PROOF. These relations are proven using Definition 6.4.1, Definition 6.4.2, and Corollary 6.4.1.

1. $\begin{cases} \alpha > 0 \Rightarrow \mu(\alpha x) = \tau(\alpha x > 0) = \tau(x > 0) = \mu(x). \\ \alpha = 0 \Rightarrow \mu(\alpha x) = \tau(0 > 0) = \tau(\text{FALSE}) = 0. \\ \alpha < 0 \Rightarrow \mu(\alpha x) = \tau(\alpha x > 0) = \tau(-x > 0) = \mu(-x). \end{cases}$

2.

$$\begin{aligned} \mu(xy) &= \tau(xy > 0) \\ &= \tau(((x > 0) \wedge (y > 0)) \vee ((x < 0) \wedge (y < 0))) \\ &= \tau((x > 0) \wedge (y > 0)) + \tau((x < 0) \wedge (y < 0)) \end{aligned}$$

$$
\begin{aligned}
&- \tau(((x > 0) \wedge (y > 0)) \wedge ((x < 0) \wedge (y < 0))) \\
&= \tau(x > 0)\tau(y > 0) + \tau(x < 0)\tau(y < 0) - \tau(\text{FALSE}) \\
&= \tau(x > 0)\tau(y > 0) + \tau(-x > 0)\tau(-y > 0) \\
&= \mu(x)\mu(y) + \mu(-x)\mu(-y).
\end{aligned}
$$

3. If $\mu(x) = 0$, then $[\mu(x)]^n = 0^n = 0 = \mu(x)$, $\forall n \in \mathbb{P}$, otherwise $\mu(x) = 1$, and $[\mu(x)]^n = 1^n = 1 = \mu(x)$. Therefore, $[\mu(x)]^n = \mu(x)$, $\forall n \in \mathbb{P}$.

4.
$$
\begin{aligned}
\mu(x)\mu(-x) &= \tau(x > 0)\tau(-x > 0) = \tau(x > 0)\tau(x < 0) \\
&= \tau((x > 0) \wedge (x < 0)) = \tau(\text{FALSE}) = 0.
\end{aligned}
$$

5. If $x > 0$ then $\mu(x) = 1$, and $max(x, 0) = x = \mu(x)x$, otherwise $\mu(x) = 0$, and $max(x, 0) = 0 = \mu(x)x$. Therefore, $\mu(x)x = max(x, 0)$.

6. This is true by Definition 6.4.2.

7. $\tau(x < 0) = \tau(-x > 0) = \mu(-x)$.

8.
$$
\begin{aligned}
\tau(x = 0) &= \tau(\overline{x < 0 \wedge x > 0}) = \tau(\overline{x < 0})\tau(\overline{x > 0}) \\
&= (1 - \tau(x < 0))(1 - \tau(x > 0)) \\
&= 1 - \tau(x < 0) - \tau(x > 0) + \tau(x < 0)\tau(x > 0) \\
&= 1 - \mu(x) - \mu(-x) + \mu(x)\mu(-x) \\
&= 1 - \mu(x) - \mu(-x) + 0 \\
&= 1 - \mu(x) - \mu(-x).
\end{aligned}
$$

9.
$$
\begin{aligned}
\tau(x \geq 0) &= \tau(\overline{x < 0}) = 1 - \tau(x < 0) = 1 - \tau(-x > 0) \\
&= 1 - \mu(-x).
\end{aligned}
$$

10. $\tau(x \leq 0) = \tau(\overline{x > 0}) = 1 - \tau(x > 0) = 1 - \mu(x)$.
11.
$$\begin{aligned} \tau(x \neq 0) &= \tau(\overline{x = 0}) = 1 - \tau(x = 0) \\ &= 1 - (1 - \mu(x) - \mu(-x)) = \mu(x) + \mu(-x). \quad \Box \end{aligned}$$

Many instances of the zero-trip problem can be solved using the above algebra.

Example **6.4.1** Suppose $s = \sum_{i=1}^{n} \sum_{j=3}^{i} \sum_{k=j}^{5} 1$.

$$s = \sum_{i=1}^{n} \sum_{j=3}^{i} \mu(6-j)(6-j).$$

On the other hand, $\mu(6-j) = 1 \Rightarrow (6-j > 0) \Rightarrow j \leq 5$. Therefore,

$$\begin{aligned} s &= \sum_{i=1}^{n} \sum_{j=3}^{\min(i,5)} (6-j) \\ &= \sum_{i=1}^{n} \mu(\min(i,5) - 2) \left(\frac{-\min^2(i,5) + 11\min(i,5) - 18}{2} \right). \end{aligned}$$

But, $\mu(\min(i,5) - 2) = 1 \Rightarrow (\min(i,5) - 2 > 0) \Rightarrow i \geq 3$. Thus,

$$\begin{aligned} s &= \sum_{i=3}^{n} \frac{-\min^2(i,5) + 11\min(i,5) - 18}{2} \\ &= \sum_{i=3}^{\min(n,5)} \frac{-i^2 + 11i - 18}{2} + \sum_{i=6}^{n} \frac{-25 + 55 - 18}{2} \\ &= \mu(\min(n,5) - 2) \left(\frac{-\min^3(n,5) + 15\min^2(n,5) - 38\min(n,5) + 24}{6} \right) \\ &\quad + \mu(n-5)6(n-5) \\ &= \mu(\min(n-2,3)) \left(\frac{-\min^3(n,5) + 15\min^2(n,5) - 38\min(n,5) + 24}{6} \right) \\ &\quad + 6\max(n-5, 0). \end{aligned}$$

TIMING ANALYSIS AND SCHEDULING

```
do i = 1, 2 * n
   do j = 1, i
      if (i + j .le. 2 * n) then
         :
      else
         :
      end if
   end do
end do
```

Figure 6.11 A loop nest with conditional statements.

Using the algebra of conditional values, a compiler may be able to obtain the probability of conditional branches inside a loop nest if the conditions are reasonably simple functions of loop index variables. This includes cases in numerical linear algebra programs where it is checked whether a particular array element lies on the lower triangle, diagonal, or upper triangle of the corresponding matrix.

Given the code segment of Figure 6.11, suppose that the compiler wants to compute the probability of the conditional branch, corresponding to the then part of the if statement in the whole iteration space of the code. That probability is equal to the ratio of the number of times that the then part is taken to the total number of times that the if statement is executed. The latter is equal to $\sum_{i=1}^{2n} \sum_{j=1}^{i} 1$, which equals to $2n^2 + n$ provided that $n > 0$.

Let the total number of times that the then part is taken be denoted by N. Then,

$$N = \sum_{i=1}^{2n} \sum_{j=1}^{i} \tau(i+j \leq 2n) = \sum_{i=1}^{2n} \sum_{j=1}^{i} \tau(i+j-2n \leq 0)$$

$$= \sum_{i=1}^{2n}\sum_{j=1}^{i}(1-\mu(i+j-2n)) = \sum_{i=1}^{2n}(\sum_{j=1}^{i}1-\sum_{j=1}^{i}\mu(i+j-2n)).$$

On the other hand, $\mu(i+j-2n) = 1 \Rightarrow (j > 2n-i)$. Therefore,

$$N = \sum_{i=1}^{2n}(\mu(i)i - \sum_{j=\max(1,2n-i+1)}^{i} 1).$$

Similarly, $(2n-i+1 \geq 1) \Rightarrow (i \leq 2n)$. Thus,

$$N = \sum_{i=1}^{2n}(\mu(i)i - \sum_{j=2n-i+1}^{i} 1) = \sum_{i=1}^{2n}(\mu(i)i - \mu(2i-2n)(2i-2n))$$
$$= \sum_{i=1}^{2n}\mu(i)i - \sum_{i=1}^{2n}\mu(2i-2n)(2i-2n).$$

But, $\mu(2i-2n) = 1 \Rightarrow \mu(i-n) = 1 \Rightarrow i > n$. Therefore,

$$N = \mu(n)2n(2n+1)/2 - \sum_{i=\max(1,n+1)}^{2n}(2i-2n).$$

On the other hand, $(n+1 \geq 1) \Rightarrow n \geq 0$. Thus,

$$N = \mu(n)n(2n+1) - 2\mu(n)\sum_{i=n+1}^{2n}(i-n)$$
$$= \mu(n)n(2n+1) - \mu(n)n(n+1) = \boxed{\mu(n)n^2}.$$

Hence, the probability that the branch corresponding to the then part is taken is equal to $\mu(n)n^2/(2n^2+n)$, which can be simplified to $\mu(n)n/(2n+1)$. In other words, if the loop is going to execute at all, then the probability of the execution of the then part of the if statement is equal to $n/(2n+1)$. Note that this probability is computed with respect to the whole iteration space of the loop nest. For a particular iteration of the outer loop, i.e. given the value of i,

TIMING ANALYSIS AND SCHEDULING

```
if (a .gt. b) then
    x = α
else
    x = 0
end if

if (b .gt. a) then
    y = β
else
    y = 0
end if

z = x * y
```

Figure 6.12 A code fragment with conditional values.

the probability that the `then` part gets executed, can be computed in a similar way. The result would be a function of `i` and `n`. This accurate branch prediction mechanism provides opportunities for a variety of optimizations based on the speculative execution approach.

Example **6.4.2** In this example we show how conditional values can be manipulated by a compiler. Consider the code fragment shown in Figure 6.12. Using the algebra of conditional values, the value of `x` after the first `if` statement is represented by $\mu(a - b)\,\alpha$. Similarly, the value of `y` after the second `if` statement will be $\mu(b - a)\,\beta$. Hence, the value of `z` will be $\mu(a - b)\,\alpha\,\mu(b - a)\,\beta$, or $\mu(a - b)\,\mu(b - a)\,\alpha\,\beta$. Corollary 6.4.2 indicates that $\mu(x)\,\mu(-x) = 0$, therefore, the value of `z` will be equal to zero.

As it is shown in the above example, the algebra of conditional values provides a mechanism for manipulation and reasoning about values of program variables. The derived closed formulas encode the control flow and data flow information, while the compiler has control over the complexity of intermediate computations. In other words, if an expressions gets more complicated than the specified tolerance, then the compiler can ignore its knowledge about that expression at that point.

7
IMPLEMENTATION AND EXPERIMENTS

The interprocedural symbolic analysis framework discussed in this book is implemented as the flow analysis scheme of Parafrase-2. Symbolic constant propagation, generalized induction expression recognition, symbolic global forward substitution, and detection of loop-invariant computations are fully implemented. All transformations and parallelization examples presented in this book, except those of Figures 6.4 and 6.5, are performed by the current version of Parafrase-2. Implementation of symbolic dependence analysis, generalized strength reduction, and symbolic timing analysis is underway. We plan to measure the effectiveness of compilation in our symbolic framework on all the codes of Perfect Benchmarks® when Parafrase-2's symbolic dependence analysis scheme is fully implemented.

We compared the current program analysis capabilities of Parafrase-2 with those of other state-of-the-art parallelizing compilers using a test suite including Perfect Benchmarks®. Other compilers considered are the 1991 version of KAP, from Kuck and Associates [Kuc88], the Titan 1500/3000 compilation system from Kubota Pacific Computer Inc., and the Alliant Fortran compiler, found in [CDL88] to be one of the best commercial vectorizers. While the Titan compiler was good at single basic block symbolic analysis, Parafrase-2 did an excellent job in a global frame. A summary of this study is shown in Table 7.1.

Table 7.1 Symbolic analysis capabilities of compilers.

Compiler Capability	Fig.	KAP	P-2	Titan	VAST-2
IVs with multiple assignments	4.9		√	√	
Linear IVs in loops with variable bounds	4.2		√		
Non-linear IVs	4.4		√		
Symbolic integer division	4.4		√		
IVs under conditional statements	4.12		√		
IVs with cyclic flow dependences	3.10		√	√	
IVs with cyclic recurrences	3.11		√		
Symbolic global forward substitution	4.4		√		
Symbolic constraint propagation	5.2		√		
Semantical loop-invariant computations	4.16		√		
Generalized induction expressions	4.6		√		
Interprocedural induction analysis	5.1		√		
IVs with dead code elimination	5.2		√		

In our experiments with Perfect Benchmarks®, we observed the need for compiler support for:

- Symbolic global forward substitution - which tries to express program expressions as functions of inputs to the program. This capability is necessary for symbolic dependence analysis.

- Symbolic constraint propagation - capability of verifying inequalities between program variables.

- Generalized induction variable and wraparound variable analysis - recognition of variables inside loops whose values can be described as closed form functions of loop index variables.

- Induction variables with multiple assignments - induction variables that are assigned more than once in loop nests.

- Computing integer division of symbolic expressions.

8
CONCLUSIONS

Existing parallelizing compilers are unable to detect and exploit effectively the available parallelism in real programs, mainly due to lack of accuracy in their analysis. The most important factor for the effective detection and management of parallelism is the precision of dependence information. Program properties that have a critical role in the dependence structure of programs are the relationships between problem size, loop bound expressions, and array subscript expressions. Accurate detection of book properties in a large class of real application programs requires advanced techniques based on computer algebra, finite differences, number theory, and theorem proving methods. Symbolic analysis can serve as a basis for an efficient compilation scheme for parallel machines by employing these analytical techniques.

8.1 FUTURE RESEARCH

The symbolic analysis techniques described in this book provide a powerful framework for solving some of the most important problems related to parallel processing; namely, the discovery and exploitation of parallelism and locality. We plan to further investigate these problems using our symbolic analysis system. As the first application, we are studying the effectiveness of the theory of loop transformations [Ban94,

Lam74], extended with the symbolic dependence information provided by our techniques.

We are also studying techniques to optimize the compilation time of programs in our framework. Currently, Parafrase-2 compiles real-life Fortran applications with an average speed of 3000 lines per wall clock minute on Sparc/10 workstations. Although this speed is cost effective, it can be further improved by employing more sparse representations suitable for symbolic analysis.

A
INTERVAL ANALYSIS

A.1 INTRODUCTION

Interval arithmetic is a generalization of real arithmetic in which intervals replace real numbers. Interval analysis[1] [Moo66] was originally developed as a tool for solving the problem of rounding error determination. By maintaining upper and lower bounds on each number during a calculation, the bounds of rounding error are determined.

Interval arithmetic takes about twice as long as ordinary arithmetic, but provides truly reliable error estimates [Knu81]. Considering the difficulty of mathematical error analysis, this is indeed a small price to pay. Unfortunately, since the intermediate values in iterative calculations often depend on each other, the final error estimates that are obtained by interval analysis tend to be overly conservative. Therefore, despite its value, in practice interval analysis is not used as often as one might expect to bound rounding errors. One notable exception is the use of interval techniques in tackling the interactable problem of *global optimization* [FP92, Han88, Han92, MHL92, RR88].

In spite of the valid criticisms of the utility of interval analysis in certain numerical applications, it cannot be denied that interval analysis is a

---
[1] Not to be confused with the interval analysis approach to flow analysis [Coc70].

coherent and systematic scheme for approximation. Hence, it is not surprising that the principal idea of interval analysis has affected the data flow analysis of programs (an inherently approximative process) and has been generalized to abstract methods for reasoning about the semantics of computer programs. In particular, the dependence analysis problem of subscripted variables, which is a constrained global optimization problem (in a small scale), can be effectively solved in practice by using enhanced interval methods. The restricted nature of the problem, especially the monotonicity of the involved functions, together with the fact that only a small number of interval operations are required for the analysis, makes interval methods perform very well in practice.

A.2 THE ORIGIN OF INTERVAL ANALYSIS

Although there were several earlier publications on the use of intervals to bound rounding errors, interval analysis was truly established as a field with the appearance of R.E.Moore's book *Interval Analysis* in 1966. Moore extended the use of interval analysis from determining the rounding errors to bounding the effects of errors from other sources, including approximation errors and errors in data. For early developments in interval arithmetic, see the appropriate references in [Knu81].

Since the appearance of Moore's book, there have been numerous publications on interval analysis [AH83, Moo79, Moo88, Nic75, Nic85]. Ratschek and Rokne's book [RR84] is a thorough discussion of the problem of finding the range of functions by using interval analysis. Moreover, several imperative languages have been extended to support the interval type [KM83, Ral83]. The computer-algebra system *Mathematica* also supports interval arithmetic [Kei95].

INTERVAL ANALYSIS

$$[a, b] + [c, d] = [a + c, b + d]$$
$$[a, b] - [c, d] = [a - d, b - c]$$
$$[a, b] * [c, d] = [\min(ac, ad, bc, bd), \max(ac, ad, bc, bd)]$$
$$[a, b]/[c, d] = [a, b] * [1/d, 1/c],\ 0 \notin [c, d]$$

Figure A.1 Interval arithmetic.

A.3 INTERVAL ARITHMETIC

Let $\mathbb{R}$ be the field of real numbers, and a and b two members of $\mathbb{R}$ such that $a \leq b$. The *closed interval* $[a, b]$ is defined to be the set of real numbers between a and b, that is,

$$[a, b] = \{x \mid a \leq x \leq b,\ x \in \mathbb{R}\}. \tag{A.1}$$

Each real number a represents a degenerate interval of the form $[a, a]$, known as a *point interval*. Two intervals are equal if they are equal in the set theoretic sense, that is, $[a, b] = [c, d] \Leftrightarrow a = c,\ b = d$. We denote the set of all closed intervals by $\mathcal{I}(\mathbb{R})$.

The arithmetic of real numbers can be generalized to interval arithmetic as follows. Let $\star \in \{+, -, *, /\}$ be a binary operation on the set of real numbers. For $A, B \in \mathcal{I}(\mathbb{R})$, the binary operation $A \star B$ is defined to be $A \star B = \{x = a \star b \mid a \in A,\ b \in B\}$ with the exception that A/B is not defined when $0 \in B$.

Since the function $f(x, y) = x \star y$, defined as above, is a continuous function on a compact set, the function $f(x, y)$ takes on a smallest and a largest value as well as all the values in between. Thus, $A \star B$ is also a closed real interval and can be calculated explicitly, as shown in Figure A.1.

By inspecting the signs of the interval bounds, the formula for interval multiplication can further be simplified by elimination of *max* and *min* functions. The following equivalent definition for interval multiplication is especially useful when the involved interval bounds are numbers (not symbolic variables), in which case the deduction of signs is trivial.

$$[a,b] * [c,d] = \begin{cases} [ac, bd] & \text{if } a \geq 0 \text{ and } c \geq 0, \\ [bc, bd] & \text{if } a \geq 0 \text{ and } c < 0 \text{ and } d > 0, \\ [bc, ad] & \text{if } a \geq 0 \text{ and } d \leq 0, \\ [ad, bd] & \text{if } a < 0 \text{ and } b > 0 \text{ and } c \geq 0, \\ [bc, ac] & \text{if } a < 0 \text{ and } b > 0 \text{ and } d \leq 0, \\ [ad, bc] & \text{if } b \leq 0 \text{ and } c \geq 0, \\ [ad, ac] & \text{if } b \leq 0 \text{ and } c < 0 \text{ and } d > 0, \\ [bd, ac] & \text{if } b \leq 0 \text{ and } d \leq 0, \\ [\min(bc, ad), & \text{if } a < 0 \text{ and } b > 0 \text{ and} \\ \quad \max(ac, bd)] & \quad c < 0 \text{ and } d > 0. \end{cases}$$

(A.2)

It follows immediately from the definition A.1 that interval addition and interval multiplication are both commutative and associative. Furthermore, the point intervals 0 and 1 are identities for interval addition and multiplication, respectively. On the other hand, the distributive law does *not* always hold for interval arithmetic. Only the so-called subdistributive law,

$$A * (B + C) \subseteq A * B + A * C, \quad A, B, C \in \mathcal{I}(\mathbb{R}), \qquad (A.3)$$

holds for interval arithmetic. For example,

$$[1, 2] * ([1, 1] - [1, 1]) = [1, 2] * [0, 0] = [0, 0],$$

whereas

$$[1, 2] * [1, 1] - [1, 2] * [1, 1] = [1, 2] - [1, 2] = [-1, 1] \supset [0, 0].$$

The distributive law is, however, valid in some special cases, for example

$$a * (B + C) = a * B + a * C, \quad a \in \mathbb{R}, \ B, C \in \mathcal{I}(\mathbb{R}),$$

INTERVAL ANALYSIS

and

$$A * (B + C) = A * B + A * C, \text{ if } bc \geq 0, \ \forall b \in B, c \in C.$$

It is emphasized that additive and multiplicative inverses exist only for point intervals. In particular, given an interval X, the interval $X - X$ is *not* necessarily the degenerate zero interval; it is zero if and only if the interval X is a point interval. This property results in widening of the intervals in interval calculations and prevents obtaining sharp results. We shall discuss this problem and the related remedies in Section A.5.

A fundamental property of interval arithmetic is the *inclusion monotonicity*. Specifically, if $A \subseteq B$ and $C \subseteq D$, then $A \star C \subseteq B \star D$, for $\star \in \{+, -, *, /\}$, with the exception that $0 \notin D$ in the case of division. It can be shown [AH83] that interval arithmetic remains inclusion monotonic even when rounding occurs, provided that outward rounding is used.

Some of the algebraic properties of interval arithmetic are summarized in Figure A.2

A.4 EXTENDED INTERVAL ARITHMETIC

In the preceding section, division by intervals containing zero was excluded. This restriction, however, can be relaxed by extending the interval arithmetic to unbounded intervals. The following formulation is due to Hansen [Han92]. Let $a, b, c,$ and d be finite values with $0 \in [c, d]$ then the rules for division by an interval containing zero are as follows.

Commutativity:	$\forall A, B \in \mathcal{I}(\mathbb{R})$, $A + B = B + A$, $A * B = B * A$.
Associativity:	$\forall A, B, C \in \mathcal{I}(\mathbb{R})$, $A + (B + C) = (A + B) + C$, $(A * B) * C = A * (B * C)$.
Subdistributivity:	$\forall A, B, C \in \mathcal{I}(\mathbb{R})$, $A * (B + C) \subseteq A * B + A * C$.
Identities:	$\forall A \in \mathcal{I}(\mathbb{R})$, $A + 0 = A$, $A * 1 = A$.
Cancellation:	$A = A + E \ \forall A \in \mathcal{I}(\mathbb{R}) \Rightarrow E = 0$, $A = A * E \ \forall A \in \mathcal{I}(\mathbb{R}) \Rightarrow E = 1$.

Figure A.2 Algebraic properties of interval arithmetic.

If $c = d$, then $[a, b]/[c, d] = (-\infty, +\infty)$, otherwise

$$[a,b]/[c,d] = \begin{cases} [b/c, +\infty) & \text{if } b \leq 0 \text{ and } d = 0, \\ (-\infty, b/d] \cup [b/c, +\infty) & \text{if } b \leq 0 \text{ and } c < 0 < d, \\ (-\infty, b/d] & \text{if } b \leq 0 \text{ and } c = 0, \\ (-\infty, +\infty) & \text{if } a < 0 \text{ and } b > 0, \\ (-\infty, a/c] & \text{if } a \geq 0 \text{ and } d = 0, \\ (-\infty, a/c] \cup [a/d, +\infty) & \text{if } a \geq 0 \text{ and } c < 0 < d, \\ [a/d, +\infty) & \text{if } a \geq 0 \text{ and } c = 0. \end{cases} \quad \text{(A.4)}$$

A.5 INTERVAL FUNCTIONS

An *interval function* of n arguments is a mapping from $\mathcal{I}^n(\mathbb{R})$ to $\mathcal{I}(\mathbb{R})$. Suppose that f is a procedure for computing a real-valued function of real variables. The interval function that is constructed from f by replacing its arguments and arithmetic operations with interval-valued arguments and the corresponding interval operations is called the *natural interval extension* of f. Computing the natural interval extension of a function yields a lower and an upper bound to the range of the function. Under certain circumstances these bounds are sharp; that is, the resulting interval indicates the maximum and minimum values of the function in the particular domain.

A.5.1 The Dependence Problem of Interval Arithmetic

Equivalent real-valued procedures may have different natural interval extensions. In other words $f(x) = g(x) \ \forall x \in \mathbb{R}$ does *not* imply that $f(X) = g(X) \ \forall X \in \mathcal{I}(\mathbb{R})$. For example, consider the real functions $f(x) = x - x$ and $g(x) = 0$. Using the axioms of real arithmetic, it is easy to show that $f(x) = g(x) \ \forall x \in \mathbb{R}$. On the other hand, by substituting $X = [a, b]$ for x in the definition of f, the natural interval extension of

f is computed as $[a, b] - [a, b]$, which is equal to $[a - b, b - a]$ by the definition of interval subtraction, shown in Figure A.1. The resulting interval is not necessarily equal to the degenerate zero interval, which is the natural interval extension of g.

Computing the positive integer powers of intervals by means of straightforward interval multiplication often yields overly conservative results. For example, consider the interval evaluation of x^2 for $X = [-a, a]$. If x^2 is interpreted as xx, the resulting interval is

$$[-a, a] * [-a, a] = [-a^2, a^2], \text{ whereas } \{x^2 | x \in [-a, a]\} = [0, a^2].$$

This loss of precision results from ignoring the *dependence* between the operands of the multiplication: the two occurrences of x have been treated as independent entities, while they are in fact identical. In general, in evaluating arbitrary interval expressions involving dependences, more accurate results can be obtained by using the existing constraints at each stage to *refine*(i.e., to tighten) the remaining intervals.

Finding a procedure that produces the narrowest possible interval for an arbitrary real-valued expression is not an easy task, given that the expression may be written in infinitely many other forms. In fact, this problem does not have a solution in its general case [RR84]. Interval analysts have spent considerable effort to find systematic methods for accurately approximating the range of real-valued functions by interval methods. A fundamental tool used in all the related techniques is the principle of *inclusion monotonicity* of interval arithmetic, which has been called *the fundamental property of interval analysis* [Han92, RR88].

The inclusion principle establishes a connection between the range of a real-valued function and its interval evaluation. It states that the natural interval extension of a real-valued function is inclusion monotone. In other words, if f is a procedure for computing a real-valued arithmetic expression then $x \in X \Rightarrow f(x) \in f(X)$. The

$$[a,b]^n = \begin{cases} [1,1] & \text{if } n = 0, \\ [a^n, b^n] & \text{if } a \geq 0, \text{ or } n \text{ is odd}, \\ [b^n, a^n] & \text{if } b < 0, \text{ and } n \text{ is even}, \\ [0, \max(a^n, b^n)] & \text{otherwise.} \end{cases}$$

Figure A.3 Integer powers of intervals.

proof [Han92, Moo66, RR84, RR88] is by induction and is based on the inclusion monotonicity of basic interval arithmetic operations.

We briefly discuss some practical techniques for improving the precision of interval computations. For a thorough treatment of the problem, see [AH83] and especially [RR84].

Powers of Intervals

For evaluating the integer powers of intervals, we shall employ the relations shown in Figure A.3 as the *definition* of exponentiation. This definition produces sharp results based on the following observation. If u is a continuous unary operation on $\mathbb{R}$, then

$$u(X) = [\min_{x \in X} u(x), \max_{x \in X} u(x)]$$

defines a subordinate unary operation on $\mathcal{I}(\mathbb{R})$ [AH83]. Examples of such unary operations on $\mathcal{I}(\mathbb{R})$ are $X^a (a \in \mathbb{R})$, $\exp X$, and $\sin X$.

Example **A.5.1** Let $f(x) = xx - 2x$ and $X = [-1, 2]$. Consider the interval evaluation of the following equivalent real-valued functions.

$$\begin{aligned}
f_0(x) &= xx - 2x \Rightarrow \\
f_0([-1,2]) &= [-1,2] * [-1,2] - 2[-1,2] = [-6,6], \\
f_1(x) &= x^2 - 2x \Rightarrow \\
f_1([-1,2]) &= [-1,2]^2 - 2[-1,2] = [-4,6], \\
f_2(x) &= x(x-2) \Rightarrow \\
f_2([-1,2]) &= [-1,2] * ([-1,2] - 2) = [-6,3], \\
f_3(x) &= (x-1)(x-1) - 1 \Rightarrow \\
f_3([-1,2]) &= ([-1,2] - 1) * ([-1,2] - 1) - 1 = [-3,3], \\
f_4(x) &= (x-1)^2 - 1 \Rightarrow \\
f_4([-1,2]) &= ([-1,2] - 1)^2 - 1 = \boxed{[-1,3]}.
\end{aligned}$$

The range of f over X is $\{x^2 - 2x | x \in [-1,2]\} = [-1,3]$. Thus, in the above list of procedures for interval computation of f over X, only f_4 yields the sharp result. Moreover, in the above list of procedures, it is only f_4 in which x occurs just once. These two facts are not independent; it can be shown [Moo66] that *for a rational expression in which each variable occurs only once, the corresponding interval evaluation will compute the actual range of the expression.*

Rewriting Arithmetic Expressions

Some of the arithmetic expressions do not have the restriction that was highlighted in Example A.5.1, namely, the property that each variable occurs only once in the expression. Yet, it might be possible to rewrite the expression in an equivalent form that satisfies that property, and thus obtain sharp results on the interval evaluation of the transformed expression.

Example **A.5.2** Let $f(x,y) = (x-y)/(x+y)$, $X = [-1,5]$, and $Y = [2,5]$. The evaluation of the natural interval extension of f over X

and Y yields

$$f([-1,5],[2,5]) = \frac{[-1,5]-[2,5]}{[-1,5]+[2,5]} = \frac{[-6,3]}{[1,10]} = [-6,3].$$

Both x and y occur more than once in the expression f. The range of f over X and Y is $[-3, 3/7]$, and the loss of precision in the interval evaluation of f results from treating the identical occurrences of x and y as independent entities. The expression f can, however, be written in the following equivalent (in real arithmetic) form:

$$f_1(x,y) = \frac{x-y}{x+y} = \frac{x+y-2y}{x+y} = 1 - \frac{2y}{x+y} = 1 - \frac{2}{1+x/y}.$$

The variables x and y occur only once in the final form of the expression f_1. Therefore, the interval evaluation of f_1 over X and Y must produce the actual range of f over X and Y.

$$\begin{aligned}
f_1([-1,5],[2,5]) &= 1 - \tfrac{2}{1+[-1,5]/[2,5]} = 1 - \tfrac{2}{1+[-1/2,5/2]} \\
&= 1 - \tfrac{2}{[1/2,7/2]} = 1 - 2[\tfrac{2}{7},2] = 1 - [\tfrac{4}{7},4] \\
&= \boxed{[-3,\tfrac{3}{7}]}.
\end{aligned}$$

In general, it is not possible to rewrite an arbitrary rational arithmetic expression in such a way that the new expression contains only one occurrence of each variable. A polynomial of second degree, however, can always be rewritten in this form. The appropriate transformation is the same as that used in Example A.5.1.

In the previous examples, it was shown that cancellation and reduction of the number of occurrences of variables can improve the precision of computing the range of real functions by interval analysis. Use of the subdistributivity law A.3can also narrow the computed intervals. Subdistributivity may, for example, be used by evaluating polynomials according to Horner's rule [Knu81]. This advantage can be observed in Example A.5.1. There, it was shown that the interval extension of $f_2(x) = x(x-2)$ produces sharper bounds than those of $f_0(x) = xx - 2x$, although f_0 and f_2 are equivalent in real arithmetic.

A.5.2 Standard Interval Forms

While in search of a candidate for a "canonical form" for interval functions, Moore [Moo66] noticed that better results (on average) are obtained when the functions are represented in a certain manner around the center of their domain. Any real-valued rational expression $f(x_1, x_2, \cdots, x_n)$ can be written in the *centered form* as

$$f_c(x_1, x_2, \cdots, x_n) = f(c_1, c_2, \cdots, c_n) + g(x_1 - c_1, x_2 - c_2, \cdots, x_n - c_n),$$

where c_i is the *center* of the interval X_i, and g is a real-valued rational expression.

For polynomials, the centered form is simply the Taylor's expansion of the function around the midpoint of the intervals. The properties of the *mean value form*, in which case c_i is not necessarily the center of X_i, have also been investigated by several authors [AH83, Moo79, RR84, RR88]. Centered forms are especially useful when the width of the involved intervals is reasonably small. Otherwise, the extra effort to use them is generally not warranted [Han92].

A.5.3 Monotonic Functions

Monotonic functions are of particular interest in interval analysis, since sharp bounds on their range can be obtained quite easily. If a real-valued function f is monotonically increasing on $[a, b]$, the range of f over $[a, b]$ is $[f(a), f(b)]$. Similarly, if f is monotonically decreasing on $[a, b]$, the range of f over $[a, b]$ is $[f(b), f(a)]$. Thus, we are able to compute sharp bounds on $f(X)$ when f is monotonic on X. Even in the presence of rounding, if outward rounding is used, we can compute $f(X)$ accurately by the above method.

Monotonicity may also be exploited even when the function is not monotonic in the entire interval. The basic idea [Moo66] is as follows. If a differentiable function f is not monotone on an interval $[a, b]$, the interval must contain at least one root of f'. The interval can further be divided into smaller subintervals in which either f is monotone or the subinterval brackets a root of f'. Interval subdivision can be done by applying a root-finding technique, such as bisecting, to f'. If f is monotonic on a subinterval, its range can be easily computed by using the method described above. Otherwise, the process of subdividing intervals continues until the width of the resulting intervals is sufficiently small, in which case the range of f can be accurately computed by interval arithmetic. The range of f over the initial interval $[a, b]$ is the *interval hull* of the range of f over the resulting subintervals.

Based on the above idea, Rall [Ral85] presents an algorithm for calculating the range of functions. The algorithm uses the information about the monotonicity of the functions obtained by automatic differentiation [Ral81].

Given the special nature of the array subscript expressions of real programs, the monotonicity test that we introduced in [HP93], and described it in detail in Section 5.2, provides an effective tool for computing the bounds of the expressions. The test does not need the derivative information and can be efficiently used in the above class of interval techniques.

A.6 INTERVALS IN AID OF PROGRAM ANALYSIS

In a pioneering work, Scott [Sco72] outlined a general theory of finite approximation for semantic interpretation of programming languages. Founded upon lattice theoretical models, this theory of functions provides a mechanism for a qualitative approach to such issues as degrees of approximation and rates of convergence to limits. Monotone and continuous lattice functions play a critical role in such an analysis.

The theory is based on the simple idea that the approximation relation $\sqsubseteq$ should be a partial ordering in which one can take limits. The relation $x \sqsubseteq y$ intuitively means that x *approximates* y or that the information contained in y includes that of x; in other words, y is more precise than x. Further considerations, such as the convenience of topological sorting in finding the limits and the ease of extending the domain of functions, bring out the necessity for the lattice structure. This structure offers a natural way for organizing information orderings.

In a lattice[2] any two elements x and y have a unique *least upper bound* (join) and a unique *greatest lower bound* (meet) denoted by $x \sqcup y$ and $x \sqcap y$, respectively. Roughly speaking, $x \sqcup y$ contains the intersection of the information of x and y, while $x \sqcap y$ holds the union of the information of x and y. Furthermore, the whole set of elements is assumed to be bounded above by an element $\top$ and bounded below by another element $\bot$. The bottom element $\bot$ stands for the "undefined" element and implies "incomplete" information, while the top element $\top$ represents the "overdefined", or somehow the "inconsistent", element.

Scott [Sco72] described in detail how Moore's interval arithmetic can be cast in the above lattice framework. Note, however, that Moore's original system [Moo66] did not have the $\top$ and $\bot$ elements and, thus, was not a lattice. In [Bir88], Birkhoff attributes the recognition of the utility of the interval concept in the far more general context of partially

---

[2] Readers interested in lattice theory are referred to [Bir67] and [DP90].

INTERVAL ANALYSIS

ordered sets to Oystein Ore's work on the foundations of abstract algebra back in 1935.

A.6.1 The Interval Lattice

Suppose that we wish to represent our information about the values of real numbers in a structure. We have the ordinary real numbers along the real line; our information at this level is exact. At the lower levels, however, we have approximations to the values of real numbers in the forms of intervals.

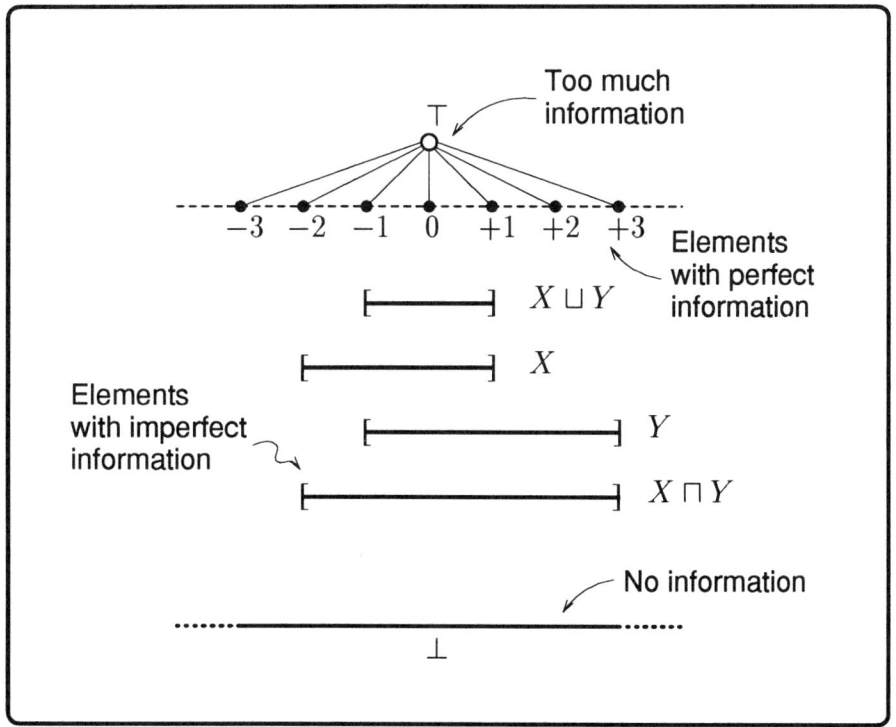

Figure A.4 The lattice $\mathbb{R}$.

One level of information is more precise than another if its corresponding interval is contained within the latter's interval. In other words,

$$x \subseteq y \Leftrightarrow x \sqsubseteq y.$$

The $\bot$ element is the infinite interval $(-\infty, +\infty)$ and carries no information. The $\top$ element which represents "too much information" is the empty set. The join of two approximations is an approximation that is at least as precise as either of the approximations. Thus, the join of two intervals can be defined as their intersection. When the intersection of two intervals is empty, the result is the overdetermined element $\top$, which indicates inconsistent information. The meet of two intervals, on the other hand, can be defined as the hull of the two intervals, which is the smallest interval that contains both of them. Figure A.4 shows the above lattice as defined by Scott [Sco72]. For other definitions of interval lattices, and their connections with continued fractions, the interested reader is referred to [Bir88].

The Cousots discussed interval analysis in the context of automatic program analysis [CC76] and introduced an abstract interpretation framework for relating various semantics of programs [CC77, CC79, Cou81]. Cousot and Halbwachs [CH78] extended the interval lattice to the lattice of convex polyhedra to discover the linear relations between program variables. Since its introduction, abstract interpretation has been an active research area, and its techniques have been applied to the analysis of several classes of programming languages. Harrison [HI89] has effectively used abstract interpretation in the automatic analysis and parallelization of functional programs.

In our study of automatic parallelization of numerical benchmarks, we attributed the failure of parallelizing compilers to their limitations in dependence analysis of cases involving unknown symbolic terms in the loop bounds and the array subscript expressions [Hag90, HP91]. In this book, and elsewhere [HP92, HP93], we introduced advanced techniques for practical symbolic analysis of programs in high-performance compilers. Recent results of Blume and Eigenmann [BE94a, BE94b, BE95] are testimonials to the importance of the role of symbolic analysis in effective automatic parallelization of programs.

For a review of the theory and various applications of abstract interpretation, the reader is referred to the collection [AH87] and the recent paper of the Cousots [CC92].

REFERENCES

[ACK81] F. E. Allen, J. Cocke, and K. Kennedy. Reduction of operator strength. In S. S. Muchnick and N. D. Jones, editors, *Program Flow Analysis*, pages 79–101. Prentice-Hall, Englewood Cliffs, New Jersey, 1981.

[AH83] G. Alefeld and J. Herzberger. *Introduction to Interval Computations*. Academic Press, New York, 1983.

[AH87] S. Abramsky and C. Hankin, editors. *Abstract Interpretation of Declarative Languages*. Ellis Horwood Limited, Chichester, West Sussex, PO19 1EB, England, 1987.

[AHI90] Z. Ammarguellat and W. L. Harrison III. Automatic recognition of induction variables and recurrence relations by abstract interpretation. In *Proceedings of the ACM SIGPLAN '90 Conference on Programming Language Design and Implementation*, pages 283–295, White Plains, New York, June 20-22 1990.

[AJ88] J. R. Allen and S. Johnson. Compiling C for vectorization, parallelization, and inline expansion. In *Proceedings of the ACM SIGPLAN '88 Conference on Programming Language Design and Implementation*, pages 241–249, Atlanta, Georgia, June 22-24 1988.

[AK87] J. R. Allen and K. Kennedy. Automatic translation of FORTRAN programs to vector form. *ACM Transactions on Programming Languages and Systems*, 9(4), October 1987.

[All70]   F. E. Allen. Control flow analysis. *ACM SIGPLAN Notices*, 5(7):1–19, July 1970.

[All83]   J. R. Allen. *Dependence analysis for subscripted variables and its application to program transformations*. PhD dissertation, Rice University, Houston, Texas, April 1983.

[AO91]   K. R. Apt and E. Olderog. *Verification of Sequential and Concurrent Programs*. Springer-Verlag, 1991.

[ASU86]   A. V. Aho, R. Sethi, and J. D. Ullman. *Compilers: Principles, Techniques and Tools*. Addison Wesley, March 1986.

[AWZ88]   B. Alpern, M. N. Wegman, and F. K. Zadeck. Detecting equality of variables in programs. In *Proceedings of the fifteenth Annual ACM SIGACT-SIGPLAN Symposium on Principles of Programming Languages*, pages 1–11, San Diego, California, January 1988.

[Ban88]   U. Banerjee. *Dependence Analysis for Supercomputing*. Kluwer, 1988.

[Ban94]   U. Banerjee. *Loop Transformations for Restructuring Compilers, Volume II: Loop Parallelization*. Kluwer, 1994.

[BE92]   W. Blume and R. Eigenmann. Performance analysis of parallelizing compilers on the Perfect benchmark programs. *IEEE Transactions on Parallel and Distributed Systems*, 3(6):643–656, November 1992.

[BE94a]   W. Blume and R. Eigenmann. An overview of symbolic analysis techniques needed for the effective parallelization of the perfect benchmarks. In *Proceedings of the 1994 ICPP*, volume II, pages 233–238, St. Charles, Illinois, August 1994.

REFERENCES

[BE94b]   W. Blume and R. Eigenmann. The range test: A dependence test for symbolic, non-linear expressions. In *Supercomputing 1994*, pages 528–537, November 1994.

[BE95]   W. Blume and R. Eigenmann. Symbolic range propagation. In *Proceedings of the 9th International Parallel Processing Symposium*, April 1995.

[Bea89]   M. Berry et al. The Perfect Club Benchmarks: Effective performance evaluation of supercomputers. *International Journal of Supercomputer Applications*, 3(3):5–40, Fall 1989.

[BF86]   I. Báráni and Z. Füredi. Computing the volume is difficult. In *18th Annual ACM Symposium on Theory of Computing*, pages 442–447, Berkeley, California, 1986.

[Bir67]   G. Birkhoff. *Lattice Theory (3rd ed.), Vol. 25*. AMS Colloquium Publications, Providence, RI, 1967.

[Bir88]   G. Birkhoff. The role of order in computing. In Moore [Moo88], pages 357–378.

[BL82]   B. Buchberger and R. Loos. Algebraic simplification. In B. Buchberger, G. E. Collins, and R. Loos, editors, *Computer Algebra: Symbolic and Algebraic Computation*, pages 11–43. Springer-Verlag, 1982.

[Blu92]   W. J. Blume. Success and limitations in automatic parallelization of the Perfect Benchmark programs. Master's thesis, Department of Computer Science, University of Illinois at Urbana-Champaign, July 1992. CSRD Report No. 1249.

[Cav70]   B. F. Caviness. On canonical forms and simplification. *Journal of the Association for Computing Machinery*, 17(2):385–396, April 1970.

[CC76]   P. Cousot and R. Cousot. Static determination of dynamic properties of programs. In B. Robinet, editor, *2nd International Symposium on Programming*, Dunod, Paris, 1976.

[CC77]   P. Cousot and R. Cousot. Abstract interpretation: A unified lattice model for static analysis of programs by construction or approximation of fixpoints. In *Proceedings of the 4th Annual ACM Symposium on Principles of Programming Languages*, pages 238–252, Los Angeles, California, January 1977.

[CC79]   P. Cousot and R. Cousot. Systematic design of program analysis frameworks. In *Proceedings of the 6th Annual ACM Symposium on Principles of Programming Languages*, pages 269–282, San Antonio, Texas, January 1979.

[CC92]   P. Cousot and R. Cousot. Abstract interpretation frameworks. *Journal of Logic and Computation*, 2(4):511–547, 1992.

[CCF91]   J. Choi, R. Cytron, and J. Ferrante. Automatic construction of sparse data flow evaluation graphs. In *Conf. Rec. 18th Annual ACM Symposium on Principles of Programming Languages*, pages 55–66. ACM, January 1991.

[CDL88]   D. Callahan, J. Dongarra, and D. Levine. Vectorizing compilers: A test suite and results. In *Supercomputing 88*, 1988.

[CFR+89]   R. Cytron, J. Ferrante, B. K. Rosen, M. N. Wegman, and F. K. Zadeck. An efficient method of computing static single assignment form. In *Conf. Rec. 16th Annual ACM Symposium on Principles of Programming Languages*, pages 25–35. ACM, January 1989.

REFERENCES

[CFR+91] R. Cytron, J. Ferrante, B. K. Rosen, M. N. Wegman, and F. K. Zadeck. Efficiently computing static single assignment form and the control dependence graph. *ACM Transactions on Programming Languages and Systems*, 13(4):451–490, October 1991.

[CFS90] R. Cytron, J. Ferrante, and V. Sarkar. Experiences using control dependence in PTRAN. In D. Gelernter, A. Nicolau, and D. A. Padua, editors, *Languages and Compilers for Parallel Processing*, pages 186–212. The MIT Press, Cambridge, Massachusetts, 1990.

[CH78] P. Cousot and N. Halbwachs. Automatic discovery of linear restraints among variables of a program. In *Proceedings of the 5th Annual ACM Symposium on Principles of Programming Languages*, pages 84–97, Tucson, Arizona, January 1978.

[CHK92] K. D. Cooper, M. W. Hall, and K. Kennedy. Procedure cloning. In *Proceedings of the Fourth IEEE International Conference on Computer Languages*, pages 96–105, Oakland, California, April 1992.

[CHT79] T. E. Cheatham, JR., H. Holloway, G., and J. A. Townley. Symbolic evaluation and the analysis of programs. *IEEE Transactions on Software Engineering*, SE-5(4):402–417, July 1979.

[CJ81a] L. A. Clarke and Richardson D. J. Symbolic evaluation methods - implementations and applications. In B. Chandrasekaran and S. Radicchi, editors, *Computer Program Testing*, pages 65–102. North-Holland, New York, 1981.

[CJ81b] L. A. Clarke and Richardson D. J. Symbolic evaluation methods for program analysis. In S. S. Muchnick and N. D. Jones, editors, *Program Flow Analysis*, pages 264–300. Prentice-Hall, Englewood Cliffs, New Jersey, 1981.

[CK77a]   J. Cocke and K. Kennedy. An algorithm for reduction of operator strength. *Communications of the Association for Computing Machinery*, 20(11):850–856, November 1977.

[CK77b]   J. Cohen and J. Katcoff. Symbolic solution of finite-difference equations. *ACM Transactions on Mathematical Software*, 3(3):261–271, September 1977.

[CL73]   C. L. Chang and R. C. T. Lee. *Symbolic Logic and Mechanical Theorem Proving*. Academic Press, 1973.

[Coc70]   J. Cocke. Global common subexpression elimination. *ACM SIGPLAN Notices*, 5(7):20–24, July 1970.

[Cou81]   P. Cousot. Semantic foundations of program analysis. In S. S. Muchnick and N. D. Jones, editors, *Program Flow Analysis*, pages 303–342. Prentice-Hall, Englewood Cliffs, New Jersey, 1981.

[CR85]   L. A. Clarke and D. J. Richardson. Applications of symbolic evaluation. *Journal of Systems and Software*, 5(1):15–35, 1985.

[CS70]   J. Cocke and J. T. Schwartz. *Programming Languages and Their Compilers*. Courant Institute of Mathematical Sciences, New York, second revised edition edition, 1970.

[DFK91]   M. Dyer, A. Frieze, and R. Kannan. A random polynomial time algorithm for approximating the volume of convex bodies. *Journal of the Association for Computing Machinery*, 38(1):1–17, January 1991.

[DJ92]   B. Dehbonei and P. Jouvelot. Semantical interprocedural analysis by partial symbolic evaluation. In *ACM SIGPLAN Workshop on Partial Evaluation and Semantics-Based Program Manipulation*, pages 14–20, San Francisco, California, June 1992.

REFERENCES

[DL93] S. K. Debray and N. W. Lin. Cost analysis of logic programs. *ACM Transactions on Programming Languages and Systems*, 15(5):826–875, November 1993.

[DMR76] M. Davis, Y. Matijasevič, and J. Robinson. Hilbert's tenth problem. Diophantine equations: Positive aspects of a negative solution. In *Mathematical Developments Arising from Hilbert Problems*, pages 323–378. American Mathematical Society, Providence, RI, 1976.

[DP90] B. A. Davey and H. A. Priestley. *Introduction to Lattices and Order*. Cambridge University Press, Cambridge, 1990.

[DST93] J. H. Davenport, Y. Siret, and E. Tournier. *Computer Algebra: Systems and Algorithms for Algebraic Computation*. Academic, second edition, 1993.

[EHJ$^+$91] R. Eigenmann, J. Hoeflinger, G. Jaxon, Z. Li, and D. A. Padua. Restructuring Fortran programs for cedar. In *Proceedings of the 1991 ICPP*, volume I, pages 57–66, St. Charles, Illinois, August 12-17 1991.

[EHLP91] R. Eigenmann, J. Hoeflinger, Z. Li, and D. A. Padua. Experience in the automatic parallelization of four Perfect-Benchmark programs. In *Proceedings of the 4th Annual Workshop on Languages and Compilers for Parallel Computing*, volume 589 of *Lecture Notes in Computer Science*, pages 65–83, Santa Clara, California, August 7-9 1991. Springer-Verlag.

[Eis71] M. Eisenberg. *Axiomatic Theory of Sets and Classes*. Holt, Rinehart and winston, Inc., New York, 1971.

[Fea88] P. Feautrier. Parametric integer programming. Technical Report 209, Laboratoire Methodlogie and Architecture Des Systems Informatiques, January 1988.

[FERN84]   J. A. Fisher, J. R. Ellis, J. C. Ruttenberg, and A. Nicolau. Parallel Processing: A Smart Compiler and A Dumb Machine. In *Conference Proceedings - The SIGPLAN '84 Symposium on Compiler Construction*, volume 19(6), pages 37–47, Montreal, Canada, June 1984.

[FFH90]   L. E. Flynn and S. Flynn Hummel. Scheduling variable-length parallel subtasks. Technical Report RC15492, IBM T.J. Watson Research Center, February 1990.

[FHSF92]   S. Flynn Hummel, E. Schonberg, and L. E. Flynn. Factoring: A method for scheduling parallel loops. *Communications of the Association for Computing Machinery*, 35(8):90–101, August 1992.

[Fie92]   J. Field. A simple rewriting semantics for realistic imperative programs and its application to program analysis. In *ACM SIGPLAN Workshop on Partial Evaluation and Semantics-Based Program Manipulation*, pages 98–107, San Francisco, California, June 1992.

[FOW87]   J. Ferrante, K. J. Ottenstein, and J. D. Warren. The program dependence graph and its use in optimization. *ACM Transactions on Programming Languages and Systems*, 9(3):319–349, July 1987.

[FP92]   C. A. Floudas and P. M. Pardalos, editors. *Recent Advances in Global Optimization*. Princeton University Press, Princeton, New Jersey, 1992.

[FU76]   A. C. Fong and J. D. Ullman. Induction variables in very high level languages. *Conf. Rec. Third ACM Symp. on Principles of Programming Languages*, pages 104–112, January 1976.

[GCL92]   K. O. Geddes, S. R. Czapor, and G. Labahn. *Algorithms for Computer Algebra*. Kluwer, 1992.

REFERENCES

[Gir91] M. B. Girkar. *Functional Parallelism : Theoretical Foundations and Implementation*. PhD dissertation, University of Illinois at Urbana-Champaign, December 1991.

[GJ78] R. W. Gosper Jr. Decision procedure for indefinite hypergeometric summation. In *Proc. Nat. Acad. Sci. 75, 1*, pages 40–42, January 1978.

[GJ79] M. R. Garey and D. S. Johnson. *Computers and Intractability, A Guide to the Theory of NP-Completeness*. W. H. Freeman, San Francisco, California, 1979.

[GJ82] T. Gonzalez and J. Ja'Ja'. Evaluation of arithmetic expressions with algebraic identities. *SIAM J. of Computing*, 11(4):633–662, November 82.

[GKP89] R. L. Graham, D. E. Knuth, and O. Patashnik. *Concrete Mathematics*. Addison-Wesley, Reading, Mass., 1989.

[GKT91] G. Goff, K. Kennedy, and C.-W. Tseng. Practical dependence testing. In *Proceedings of the ACM SIGPLAN '91 Conference on Programming Language Design and Implementation*, pages 15–29, Toronto, Ontario, Canada, June 26-28 1991.

[GP88] M. Girkar and C. D. Polychronopoulos. Compiling issues for supercomputers. In *Supercomputing 88*, pages 164–173. IEEE Computer Society Press, 1988.

[GP92] M. Girkar and C. D. Polychronopoulos. The HTG: An intermediate representation for programs based on control and data dependences. *IEEE Transactions on Parallel and Distributed Systems*, 3(2):166–178, March 1992.

[GT93] D. Grove and L. Torczon. Interprocedural constant propagation: A study of jump function implementation. In *Proceedings of the ACM SIGPLAN '93 Conference on Programming Language Design and Implementation*, pages 90–99, Albuquerque, New Mexico, June 1993.

[Hag90]   M. R. Haghighat. Symbolic dependence analysis for high performance parallelizing compilers. Master's thesis, Department of Computer Science, University of Illinois at Urbana-Champaign, Urbana, Illinois, May 1990. CSRD Report No. 995.

[Han88]   E. R. Hansen. An overview of global optimization using interval analysis. In Moore [Moo88], pages 289–305.

[Han92]   E. R. Hansen. *Global Optimization Using Interval Analysis*. Marcel Dekker, New York, 1992.

[Hav93]   P. Havlak. Construction of thinned gated single-assignment form. In *Proceedings of the 6th Annual Workshop on Languages and Compilers for Parallel Computing*, volume 768 of *Lecture Notes in Computer Science*, pages 477–499, Portland, Oregon, August 1993. Springer-Verlag.

[Hav94]   P. Havlak. *Interprocedural Symbolic Analysis*. PhD dissertation, Department of Computer Science, Rice University, 1994.

[HC88]   T. Hickey and J. Cohen. Automating program analysis. *Journal of the Association for Computing Machinery*, 35(1):185–220, January 1988.

[Hec77]   M. S. Hecht. *Flow Analysis of Computer Programs*. Elsevier North-Holland, 1977.

[HI89]   W. L. Harrison III. *The Interprocedural Analysis and Automatic Parallelization of Scheme Programs*. PhD dissertation, University of Illinois, February 1989.

[HK91]   P. Havlak and K. Kennedy. An implementation of interprocedural bounded regular section analysis. *IEEE Transactions on Parallel and Distributed Systems*, 2(3):350–360, 1991.

[HMCCR93] M. W. Hall, J. Mellor-Crummey, A. Carle, and R. G. Rodríguez. FIAT: A framework for interprocedural analysis and transformations. In *Proceedings of the 6th Annual Workshop on Languages and Compilers for Parallel Computing*, volume 768 of *Lecture Notes in Computer Science*, pages 522–545, Portland, Oregon, August 1993. Springer-Verlag.

[HP91] M. R. Haghighat and C. D. Polychronopoulos. Symbolic dependence analysis for high-performance parallelizing compilers. In A. Nicolau, D. Gelernter, T. Gross, and D. A. Padua, editors, *Advances in Languages and Compilers for Parallel Processing*, pages 310–330. The MIT Press, Cambridge, Massachusetts, 1991.

[HP92] M. R. Haghighat and C. D. Polychronopoulos. Symbolic program analysis and optimization for parallelizing compilers. In *Proceedings of the 5th Annual Workshop on Languages and Compilers for Parallel Computing*, volume 757 of *Lecture Notes in Computer Science*, pages 538–562, New Haven, Connecticut, August 1992. Springer-Verlag.

[HP93] M. R. Haghighat and C. D. Polychronopoulos. Symbolic analysis: A basis for parallelization, optimization, and scheduling of programs. In *Proceedings of the 6th Annual Workshop on Languages and Compilers for Parallel Computing*, volume 768 of *Lecture Notes in Computer Science*, pages 567–585, Portland, Oregon, August 1993. Springer-Verlag.

[HP94] M. R. Haghighat and C. D. Polychronopoulos. Symbolic analysis for parallelizing compilers. *Submitted to ACM Transactions on Programming Languages and Systems*, 1994.

[Hun74] T. W. Hungerford. *Algebra*. Springer-Verlag, 1974.

[Iri93] F. Irigoin. Interprocedural analyses for programming environments. In J. J. Dongarra and B. Tourancheau, editors, *Environments and Tools for Parallel Scientific Computing*, pages 333–350. Elsevier Science, 1993.

[Ivi78] J. Ivie. Some MACSYMA programs for solving recurrence relations. *ACM Transactions on Mathematical Software*, 4(1):24–33, March 1978.

[JD89] P. Jouvelot and B. Dehbonei. A unified semantic approach for the vectorization and parallelization of generalized reductions. In *Proceedings of the 1989 International Conference on Supercomputing*, Crete, Greece, June 5-9 1989.

[JGS93] N. D. Jones, C. K. Gomard, and P. Sestoft. *Partial Evaluation and Automatic Program Generation*. Prentice-Hall, 1993.

[JM91] J. P. Jones and Y. Matijasevič. Proof of recursive unsolvability of Hilbert's tenth problem. *The American Mathematical Monthly*, 98(8):689–709, October 1991.

[Jor65] C. Jordan. *Calculus of Finite Differences*. Chelsea, New York, third edition, 1965.

[Jou87] P. Jouvelot. Semantic parallelization: A practical exercise in abstract interpretation. In *Proceedings of the Fourteenth Annual ACM Symposium on Principles of Programming Languages*, pages 39–48, Munich, West Germany, January 1987.

[Kar81] M. Karr. Summation in finite terms. *Journal of the Association for Computing Machinery*, 28(2):305–350, April 1981.

[Kei95] J. B. Keiper. Interval arithmetic in Mathematica. *The Mathematica Journal*, 5(2):66–71, Spring 1995.

REFERENCES

[Ken81] K. Kennedy. A survey of data flow analysis techniques. In S. S. Muchnick and N. D. Jones, editors, *Program Flow Analysis*, pages 5–54. Prentice-Hall, Englewood Cliffs, New Jersey, 1981.

[Kil73] G. A. Kildall. A unified approach to global program optimization. *Conf. Rec. First ACM Symp. on Principles of Programming Languages*, pages 194–206, 1973.

[KKLW80] D. J. Kuck, R. H. Kuhn, B. Leasure, and M. J. Wolfe. The structure of an advanced vectorizer for pipelined processors. In *Fourth International Computer Software and Applications Conference*, October 1980.

[KM83] U. W. Kulisch and W. L. Miranker, editors. *A New Approach to Scientific Computation*. Academic Press, New York, 1983.

[Knu73] D. E. Knuth. *The Art of Computer Programming, Vol. 1 / Fundamental Algorithms*. Addison-Wesley, Reading, Mass., second edition, 1973.

[Knu81] D. E. Knuth. *The Art of Computer Programming, Vol. 2 / Seminumerical Algorithms*. Addison-Wesley, Reading, Mass., second edition, 1981.

[Knu92] D. E. Knuth. Two notes on notation. *The American Mathematical Monthly*, 99(5):403–422, May 1992.

[Koz81] D. Kozen. Semantics of probabilistic programs. *Journal of Computer and System Sciences*, 22(3):328–350, June 1981.

[Kuc88] Kuck & Associates, Inc., Champaign, Illinois. *KAP User's Guide*, 1988.

[KW85] C. Kruskal and A. Weiss. Allocating independent subtasks on parallel processors. *IEEE Transactions on Software Engineering*, SE-11(10), October 1985.

[Lam74] L. Lamport. The parallel execution of DO loops. *Communications of the Association for Computing Machinery*, 17(2):83–93, February 1974.

[Lea85] B. Leasure. The Parafrase project's Fortran analyzer major module documentation. Technical report, Center for Supercomputing Research and Development, University of Illinois, 1985. CSRD Report No. 504.

[LT88] A. Lichnewsky and F. Thomasset. Introducing symbolic problem solving techniques in the dependence testing phases of a vectorizer. In *Supercomputing 88*. IEEE Computer Society Press, July 1988.

[Mat93] IU. V. Matiiasevich. *Hilbert's Tenth Problem*. MIT Press, Cambridge, Massachusetts, 1993.

[MHL91] D. E. Maydan, J. L. Hennessy, and M. S. Lam. Efficient and exact data dependence analysis. In *Proceedings of the ACM SIGPLAN '91 Conference on Programming Language Design and Implementation*, pages 1–14, Toronto, Ontario, Canada, June 26-28 1991.

[MHL92] R. E. Moore, E. R. Hansen, and A. Leclerc. Rigorous methods for global optimization. In Floudas and Pardalos [FP92], pages 321–342.

[Moo66] R. E. Moore. *Interval Analysis*. Prentice-Hall, Englewood Cliffs, New Jersey, 1966.

[Moo79] R. E. Moore. *Methods and Applications of Interval Analysis*. SIAM, Philadelphia, 1979.

[Moo88] R. E. Moore, editor. *Reliability in Computing: The Role of Interval Methods in Scientific Computing*. Academic Press, New York, 1988.

[Mor95] J. E. Moreira. *On the Implementation and Effectiveness of Autoscheduling for Shared-Memory Multiproces-*

sors. PhD dissertation, University of Illinois at Urbana-Champaign, Urbana, Illinois, February 1995.

[Mos71]   J. Moses. Algebraic simplification: A guide for the perplexed. *Communications of the Association for Computing Machinery*, 14(8):527–537, August 1971.

[Nic75]   K. Nickel, editor. *Proceedings of the International Symposium on Interval Mathematics*, volume 29 of *Lecture Notes in Computer Science*, Karlsruhe, Germany, May 1975. Springer-Verlag.

[Nic85]   K. Nickel, editor. *Proceedings of the International Symposium on Interval Mathematics*, volume 212 of *Lecture Notes in Computer Science*, Freiburg i.Br., Germany, September 1985. Springer-Verlag.

[NZM91]   I. Niven, H. S. Zuckerman, and H. L. Montgomery. *An Introduction to the Theory of Numbers*. John Wiley and Sons, New York, fifth edition, 1991.

[Pai81]   R. Paige. *Formal Differentiation: A Program Synthesis Technique*. UMI Research Press, Ann Arbor, Michigan, 1981.

[PGH+89]   C. D. Polychronopoulos, M. B. Girkar, M. R. Haghighat, C. L. Lee, B. P. Leung, and D. A. Schouten. Parafrase-2: An environment for parallelizing, partitioning, synchronizing and scheduling programs on multiprocessors. In *Proceedings of the 1989 ICPP*, volume II, pages 39–48, St. Charles, Illinois, August 1989.

[PK87]   C. D. Polychronopoulos and D. J. Kuck. Guided self-scheduling: A practical scheduling scheme for parallel computers. *IEEE Transactions on Computers*, C-36(12):1425–1439, December 1987.

[Pol88]   C. D. Polychronopoulos. *Parallel Programming and Compilers*. Kluwer, 1988.

[PS77]   R. Paige and J. T. Schwartz. Expression continuity and the formal differentiation of algorithms. In *Proceedings of the 4th Annual ACM Symposium on Principles of Programming Languages*, pages 58–71, Los Angeles, California, January 1977.

[PTTF92] W. H. Press, S. A. Teukolsky, Vetterling W. T., and B. P. Flannery. *Numerical Recipes in FORTRAN: The Art of Scientific Computing*. Cambridge University Press, second edition, 1992.

[Pug91] W. Pugh. The Omega test: A fast and practical integer programming algorithm for dependence analysis. In *Supercomputing 91*, 1991.

[PW86]   D. A. Padua and M. J. Wolfe. Advanced compiler optimizations for supercomputers. *Communications of the ACM*, 29(12):1184–1201, December 1986.

[Ral81] L. B. Rall. *Automatic Differentiation: Techniques and Applications*, volume 120 of *Lecture Notes in Computer Science*. Springer-Verlag, 1981.

[Ral83] L. B. Rall. Differentiation and generation of Taylor coefficients in pascal-sc. In Kulisch and Miranker [KM83], pages 291–309.

[Ral85] L. B. Rall. Improved interval bounds for range of functions. In Nickel [Nic85], pages 143–155.

[Ram79] L. H. Ramshaw. Formalizing the analysis of algorithms. Technical Report SL-79-5, Xerox Palo Alto Research Center, Palo Alto, California, 1979.

[Rei80] J. H. Reif. Code motion. *SIAM J. of Computing*, 9(2):375–395, May 1980.

[Ric68] D. Richardson. Some unsolvable problems involving elementary functions of a real variable. *Journal of Symbolic Logic*, 33:511–520, 1968.

REFERENCES

[RL77] J. H. Reif and Harry R. Lewis. Symbolic evaluation and the global value graph. *Conf. Rec. Fourth ACM Symp. on Principles of Programming Languages*, pages 104–118, January 1977.

[RL86] J. H. Reif and H. R. Lewis. Efficient symbolic analysis of programs. *Journal of Computer and System Sciences*, 32(3):280–314, June 1986.

[RR84] H. Ratschek and J. Rokne. *Computer Methods for the Range of Functions*. Ellis Horwood Limited, Chichester, West Sussex, PO19 1EB, England, 1984.

[RR88] H. Ratschek and J. Rokne. *New Computer Methods for Global Optimization*. Ellis Horwood Limited, Chichester, West Sussex, PO19 1EB, England, 1988.

[RT81] J. H. Reif and R. E. Tarjan. Symbolic program analysis in almost linear time. *SIAM J. of Computing*, 11(1):81–93, February 81.

[RWZ88] B. K. Rosen, M. N. Wegman, and F. K. Zadeck. Global value numbers and redundant computations. In *Proceedings of the fifteenth Annual ACM SIGACT-SIGPLAN Symposium on Principles of Programming Languages*, pages 12–27, San Diego, California, January 1988.

[Sar89a] V. Sarkar. Determining average program execution times and their variance. In *Proceedings of the ACM SIGPLAN '89 Conference on Programming Language Design and Implementation*, pages 298–312, Portland, Oregon, June 21-23 1989.

[Sar89b] V. Sarkar. *Partitioning and Scheduling Parallel Programs for Multiprocessors*. The MIT Press, Cambridge, Massachusetts, 1989.

[Sch90] D. A. Schouten. An overview of interprocedural analysis techniques for high performance parallelizing compilers.

Master's thesis, Department of Computer Science, University of Illinois at Urbana-Champaign, Urbana, 1990. CSRD Report No. 1005.

[Sco72] D. Scott. Lattice theory, data types and semantics. In R. Rustin, editor, *Formal Semantics of Programming Languages*, pages 65–106. Prentice-Hall, Englewood Cliffs, New Jersey, 1972.

[SH92] J. P. Singh and J. L. Hennessy. An empirical investigation of the effectiveness and limitations of automatic parallelization. In N. Suzuki, editor, *Shared Memory Multiprocessing*, pages 213–240. MIT Press, Cambridge, Massachusetts, 1992.

[Sin72] M. Sintzoff. Calculating properties of programs by valuations on specific models. In *SIGPLAN Notices 7 (1), Proceedings of an ACM Conference on Proving Assertions About Programs*, pages 203–207. ACM, January 1972.

[TIF86] R. Triolet, F. Irigoin, and P. Feautrier. Direct parallelization of Call statements. In *Proceedings of the SIGPLAN '86 Symposium on Compiler Construction*, Palo Alto, California, 1986.

[TN91] T. H. Tzen and L. M. Ni. Dynamic loop scheduling for shared memory multiprocessors. In *Proceedings of the 1991 ICPP*, volume 2, St. Charles, Illinois, August 1991.

[TY86] P. Tang and P.-C. Yew. Processor self-scheduling for multiple-nested parallel loops. In *Proceedings of the 1986 ICPP*, St. Charles, Illinois, August 1986.

[Ull73] J. D. Ullman. Fast algorithms for the elimination of common subexpressions. *Acta Informatica*, 2:3:191–213, July 1973.

REFERENCES

[Weg75a]   B. Wegbreit. Mechanical program analysis. *Communications of the Association for Computing Machinery*, 18(9):528–539, September 1975.

[Weg75b]   B. Wegbreit. Property extraction in well-founded property sets. *IEEE Transactions on Software Engineering*, 1(3):270–285, September 1975.

[Weg76a]   B. Wegbreit. Goal-directed program transformation. *IEEE Transactions on Software Engineering*, SE-2(2):69–80, June 1976.

[Weg76b]   B. Wegbreit. Verifying program performance. *Journal of the Association for Computing Machinery*, 23(4):691–699, October 1976.

[Wol78]   M. J. Wolfe. Techniques for improving the inherent parallelism in programs. Technical Report 78-929, Department of Computer Science, University of Illinois at Urbana-Champaign, July 1978.

[Wol89]   M. J. Wolfe. *Optimizing Supercompilers for Supercomputers*. The MIT Press, Cambridge, Massachusetts, 1989.

[Wol90]   M. J. Wolfe. Flow graph anomalies: What's in a loop? Technical report, Oregon Graduate Institute, Beaverton, Oregon, 1990.

[Wol92]   M. J. Wolfe. Beyond induction variables. In *Proceedings of the ACM SIGPLAN '92 Conference on Programming Language Design and Implementation*, pages 162–174, San Francisco, California, June 17-19 1992.

[Wol93]   M. J. Wolfe. Engineering a data dependence test. *Concurrency: Practice and Experience*, 5(7):603–622, October 1993.

[WZ84]   M. N. Wegman and F. K. Zadeck. Constant propagation with conditional branches. *Journal of the Association for Computing Machinery*, pages 291–299, 1984.

[WZ85]   M. N. Wegman and F. K. Zadeck. Constant propagation with conditional branches. In *Proceedings of Twelfth POPL*, pages 291–299, January 1985.

[WZ91]   M. N. Wegman and F. K. Zadeck. Constant propagation with conditional branches. *ACM Transactions on Programming Languages and Systems*, 13(2):181–210, April 1991.

[ZC91]   H. P. Zima and B. M. Chapman. *Supercompilers for Parallel and Vector Computers*. ACM Press, New York, 1991.

INDEX

Abstract interpretation, 1, 5–7, <u>9</u>, 12–13, 21, 23, 25, 28–29, 58, 110, 112–113
Birth point, <u>21</u>–23
Canonical system, <u>10</u>, 13
  recursive, 10
  sparse distributive, 10
Conditional values, 83–<u>84</u>, 89, 91
Constant propagation, 5–6, 64
Control flow graph interpretation, 14, <u>21</u>
Cost analysis, see Timing analysis
Dependence analysis, 2–3, 38, 46, 55, 59, 61, 63–**64**, 64–**65**, 94
Dependence problem of interval arithmetic, <u>103</u>–104
Dependence tests, 54, 64–65
Elimination of dead-code, 6, 36, **50**, <u>61</u>, 63, 65
Finite differences, 19, 29, 46–47, 54, 66
Functional behavior of programs, 23
Hierarchical Task Graph, 21, 58, 72

Inclusion monotonicity, 101, 104–105
Induction variables, <u>35</u>
  characteristic function, <u>40</u>, 42, 44
  conditional, 50, 79–80
  coupled, 29, 42, **44**, 94
  expressions, <u>40</u>
  generalized, <u>37</u>, <u>40</u>, 93–94
  geometric, 37, 46
  linear, 35–**37**, 47
  non-linear, **40**, 79
  periodic, 54
  recursive, 29
  substitution, <u>36</u>
  wraparound, 37, <u>51</u>–**53**, 94
Integer arithmetic, <u>9</u>
Integral domain, 9–10
Interprocedural symbolic analysis, 1–4, 7, **59**, **61**
Interval analysis, <u>97</u>
  centered form, <u>108</u>
  closed interval, 99
  dependence problem, 103–104
  extended interval arithmetic, 101
  fundamental property, <u>104</u>
  interval arithmetic, <u>99</u>

interval extension, 103–104
interval functions, 103
lattice, <u>111</u>
mean value form, <u>108</u>
origin, 98
point interval, <u>99</u>, 101
powers of intervals, 104–<u>105</u>
range of functions, 98,
  103–104, **106**–<u>108</u>, 109
rewriting expressions, 106
standard forms, 108
subdistributive law, <u>100</u>, <u>107</u>
widening of intervals, 101
KAP preprocessor, <u>2</u>, 44, 93
Loop-invariant computations,
  2–3, 47, 55–56, 93
Loops, <u>23</u>
  analysis, <u>28</u>
  back edge, 23
  bounds normalization, <u>54</u>
  header, 23
  natural, 23
  nesting, <u>25</u>
  structure normalization, 25,
    58
Monotonic functions, 64,
  66–67, 98, 108–109
Monotonicity test, <u>64</u>, 109
Newton's expansion, 18–19
Newton's interpolation
  formula, 47–48
Parafrase-2, <u>1</u>, 4, 23, 25, 29,
  32–33, 37–38, 40, 43–44,
  46–47, 50–56, 59, 61, 78,
  80, 93, 96

Perfect Benchmarks, <u>1</u>, 37, 42,
  44, 47, 51–52, 63, 93–94
Performance prediction, see
  Timing analysis
Recurrence relations, 7, <u>24</u>,
  28–29, 59
Scheduling, 72
  load balancing, 72
  parallel loops, 72, 75–76
    balanced chunk scheduling,
    73–<u>74</u>
Strength reduction, 6, <u>36</u>, 56
  generalized, <u>68</u>, 72, 75–76, 93
Structural conditions, 71, 80, <u>82</u>
  branch prediction, 91
Symbolic analysis system
  analyzer, <u>58</u>
  architecture, <u>56</u>
  interpreter, <u>58</u>
  kernel, <u>58</u>
Symbolic constant propagation,
  2, 61, 93
Symbolic constraint
  propagation, 29, 31, 49, 94
Symbolic dependence analysis,
  61, <u>63</u>–**64**, 64, 98, 112
Symbolic divisibility test, 16,
  20, 38, 94
  limited inspection, <u>18</u>
  mathematical induction, <u>17</u>
Symbolic division, 10, 15
Symbolic domain, <u>13</u>, 15, 56
Symbolic forward substitution,
  38, 43, 93–94

Symbolic interpolation, 46–47, 53
Timing analysis, 3, 71, 73–74, 76, <u>78</u>, **80**
Titan compiler, <u>2</u>, 7, 46, 93
Undecidability
  Hilbert's tenth problem, 31
  induction variables recognition, 41
  loop termination, 30
VAST-2 preprocessor, <u>2</u>, 93
Zero equivalence problem, 10
Zero-trip loops, 32, <u>82</u>, 88